people
in
bondage

people in bondage

African Slavery in the Modern Era

L. H. Ofosu-Appiah

Director, Encyclopaedia Africana

Lerner Publications Company
Minneapolis, Minnesota

ACKNOWLEDGMENTS

The illustrations are reproduced through the courtesy of: pp. 6, 28, 30, 44, 48, 49, 52, 56, 81, 97, 102, 106, 116, Independent Picture Service; p. 9, Kunsthistorischen Museums, Vienna; pp. 11, 104-105, Jay P. Altmayer Collection; p. 13, Museo del Prado, Madrid; p. 14, Musée Condé, Chantilly, Photo Giraudon; pp. 19, 26, 46, 69, British Museum; pp. 20, 24, 46, 85, 94, National Maritime Museum, Greenwich; pp. 22, 60, The Viking Press, Inc.; p. 29, The American Numismatic Society; p. 34, The Peabody Museum of Salem; pp. 35, 123, New York Public Library, Schomburg Collection; p. 37, Museum of Fine Arts, Boston; pp. 38, 40, 73, 75, 78, 100, 113 (left), 119, Library of Congress; pp. 54-55, Radio Times Hulton Picture Library; p. 62, Charleston Library Society; p. 71, The Anti-Slavery Society, London; p. 77, The Virginia Museum of Fine Arts; p. 80, Josiah Wedgwood and Sons Ltd.; p. 83, National Portrait Gallery, London; p. 88, The Pennsylvania Academy of the Fine Arts; p. 108, State Department of Archives and History, Raleigh, N.C.; p. 110, The New York Historical Society; p. 113 (right), Smith College Library; p. 114, Cincinnati Art Museum; pp. 125, 128, United Press International, Inc.; p. 126, Wide World Photos.

The Library of Congress cataloged the
original printing of this title as follows:

Ofosu-Appiah, L. H.
    People in bondage; African slavery in the modern era [by]
L. H. Ofosu-Appiah. Minneapolis, Minn., Lerner Publications
Co. [1971]

    131 p. illus., facsims., maps, ports. 23 cm.

SUMMARY: A history of the slave trade from ancient and
medieval times to its abolition after the Civil War.

    1. Slave trade—Africa—Juvenile literature. 2. Slave trade—
Juvenile literature. [1. Slave trade. 2. Slavery] I. Title.

HT1321.O28   326'.096   70-128799
ISBN 0-8225-0624-6   MARC

                                                  AC

International Standard Book Number: 0-8225-0624-6
Library of Congress Catalog Card Number: 70-128799

Second Printing 1972

Contents

Columbus's landing on San Salvador in 1492 marked the beginning of a new and terrible era in the history of slavery. The European discovery of a vast new world in the Western Hemisphere created a demand for black slaves which would last for almost four centuries.

1

Slavery in the Ancient and Medieval Worlds

The institution of slavery has had a very long and disgraceful history. It has probably existed at some time in all human communities where physical work on the land was required. Extended by wars of conquest and by the growth of empires, slavery eventually became an accepted part of life in most human societies.

The origin of the word slave sheds some light on the history of slavery as a human institution. The English word is derived from the Old French *esclave,* which comes from the Medieval Latin word for slave, *sclavus.* According to the Oxford Universal Dictionary, *sclavus* was also the Latin name for the people known today as Slavs, inhabitants of Eastern Europe such as the Russians, Bulgarians, Poles, Czechs, and Yugoslavs, whose languages have common Slavic roots. Historians tell us that the Slavs were originally a barbarian tribe driven out of their homes by the nomad Avars, who left the Eurasian steppe to destroy the Roman Empire. The nomads needed food, so they turned the Slavs into slaves to work the land for them.

In the Middle Ages the Slavic people were again enslaved by a foreign power, this time by the Moorish rulers in Spain. The Ummayyad caliphs of Cordova maintained a slave bodyguard which their Frankish neighbors recruited for them. The Franks (the ancestors of the modern French) supplied the Cordovan caliphs with slaves by raiding the lands adjacent to the Frankish kingdom. The barbarians of those lands happened to be Slavs whom the Avars had earlier dominated.

Thus, through an accident of history, the word designating the Slavs as a people gradually came to refer to any person sold into servitude and owned by another. The interesting feature of this historical evidence is that in the early stages of the history of slavery the color of the slave's skin was not significant. There were slaves of all nationalities and colors. The only basis for enslavement was the principle "Might is right."

Slavery was widespread in most ancient societies. It existed in ancient Egypt, China, India, Peru, and Mexico and was the mainstay of the Greek and Roman civilizations. In the Old Testament slavery is an accepted institution. The law and morality of the ancient world sanctioned slavery, and societies which practiced it did not believe that they were doing something cruel and inhuman. However, rulers took care to ensure that they themselves would not be enslaved and always took stern measures against slave uprisings.

All the world's great religions have supported slavery

In most ancient societies slaves were acquired primarily through military conquest. This cameo from the first century B.C. shows the Roman emperor Augustus being crowned with the laurel wreath of victory in recognition of his triumph over a German army. In the lower half of the cameo, Roman soldiers bind German war captives who will be sold as slaves.

at some time. In the Middle Ages and the modern era, the established churches in Europe and the Americas approved the existence of slavery within their areas of influence. The Roman Catholic Church sanctioned the enslaving of Indians and Negroes in the West Indies and South America, and the Anglican Church was a staunch supporter of the institution in the English colonies. When Islam became a world religion, it too gave its blessing to the enslavement of men of many nations and religions.

Historically, the great religions of the world have not led the way in reducing the brutality of man to man. In fact, they have sometimes encouraged slavery by claiming divine support for it. The Christians in Europe and America had a simple way of rationalizing this cruel system. They took for granted that the Christian religion was morally superior to any pagan religion. From this standpoint they argued that it was in the interest of the pagan slave to become the property of a Christian, presumably because the brutality of Christians was kindness compared to the spiritual hardships of the pagan's life.

Throughout history the most common methods of enslavement have been conquest by war, kidnapping, piracy, and the custom of selling persons unable to pay debts. Under most systems of slavery the children born of slave parents also became slaves. In ancient, medieval, and modern societies the lot of slaves has always varied. All slaves were deprived of their freedom, but the conditions of their servitude depended on the work required of them and the society in which they lived. The work done by slaves has varied from hard plantation labor and domestic chores to soldiering, educational and administrative duties, and the ruling of states in empires.

Of all the kinds of slavery practiced throughout history, plantation slavery was without doubt the most brutal; it affected the character of both masters and slaves. The nature of the plantation system, which was designed to produce cash crops on a large scale, made it almost impossible for the slave owner to regard the slave as a human being. Aristotle's definition of a slave as "a tool that breathes" aptly describes the kind of existence endured by those enslaved under this system. (It is significant to note

*A 19th-century cotton plantation in the southern United States. Planta-
tion slavery was the most common form of slavery in the New World.
Slaves also worked on large plantations or estates in Italy and Sicily
during the Roman era.*

that the system of slavery most common in the United
States during the 19th century was plantation slavery.)

Another type of slavery, practiced mainly by the Ottoman Turks, differed considerably from the usual pattern.
The Ottoman Turks were nomadic people who established
a vast empire in the Near East during the late Middle Ages.
Historically, when nomads conquered a territory, they
merely enslaved the inhabitants and used them for working
the land. This custom made it easy for the slaves to rise
after a time and overthrow their lords. Consequently, most
nomad empires did not last long. The Ottoman Turks
adopted a different method; they used slaves for important

positions in the government, the army, and the court. From the time of Suleiman the Magnificent, who reigned from 1520 to 1566, everyone who came into the sultan's service was considered the sultan's slave. The elite Ottoman army corps, called the Janissaries, was made up largely of slaves and war captives who had been converted to Islam. Negro slaves, who were not permitted in the army, generally served as eunuchs in the sultan's harem. (A eunuch is a man whose external sexual organs have been removed.) The Chief Eunuch at the Ottoman court was a very powerful official who possessed his own seal of office.

The unique aspect of the Ottoman system of slavery was that in it slaves could achieve power and influence; all those who were prepared to be educated could aspire to positions of trust. Slaves became full citizens in such situations and so ceased for all practical purposes to be slaves. However, the fact of their slave origin was not forgotten.

In Ottoman society, slaves often held positions of importance in the government and the army. In another part of the medieval Muslim world, a slave dynasty actually ruled for more than 250 years. This unusual development took place in Egypt. Turkish slaves called Mamluks (or Mamelukes) had been used as soldiers by the Arab sultans of Egypt from the 10th century on. The slave army became so powerful that in 1250 it was able to overthrow the government and set up one of its own leaders as sultan. The Mamluks ruled Egypt until 1517, when the Ottoman Turks defeated them and seized control. Even under Ottoman rule, however, the Mamluk warriors retained much of their influence and military strength. At the end of the 18th century, they were still powerful enough to organize an

After the Mamluk warriors were defeated by Napoleon in 1798, some of them joined the French army. In this painting the Spanish artist Francisco Goya shows Mamluk soldiers, led by a French officer, fighting during Napoleon's invasion of Spain in 1808.

army in an attempt to defend Egypt against Napoleon's invasion. Napoleon defeated the Mamluks but their power was not completely crushed until 1811, when the Turkish governor of Egypt, Mohammed Ali, had them exterminated.

During the Middle Ages, European peasants, or serfs, lived under a system of bondage that was similar to slavery in some ways. A serf was generally bound to the land and was required to work for the lord of the manor.

The rise and fall of the Mamluk slave dynasty is a fascinating episode in the history of slavery, but it is hardly typical of the fate of most enslaved people. The majority of slaves, by virtue of their condition, had little opportunity to attain power or position. A slave, by definition, is the property of another human being. He is like a sheep or goat owned by a man and, like a domestic animal, is subject to his master's will. Under rigid systems of slavery the slave's right to own property was strictly limited or nonexistent. In most slave-owning societies masters had the power of life and death over their slaves, and excessive flogging was a normal punishment. Slaves were often branded with hot irons to make sure that those who ran away could be identified.

In some societies slaves did have the means of acquiring their freedom; they could purchase it or be freed by the master or by the law. A slave who gained his freedom became a freedman and acquired certain rights. Citizenship for the freedman, however, was a privilege and not a right.

The characteristics outlined above do not pertain to the type of slaves used by the Ottoman Turks to run their empire, but they do apply to slaves in most countries which had a long tradition of slavery. In such societies a slave was distinguished from an animal only by the fact that he could speak and perform other functions which normal human beings could perform. Unlike other men, however, he was not expected to think for himself. The slave owners in these societies knew that most slaves wanted their freedom, so they usually made elaborate provisons for the punishment of runaway slaves. Much of the brutality traditionally connected with slavery was meant to frighten the enslaved into submission. That these measures often failed is clear from the number of slave revolts in recorded history.

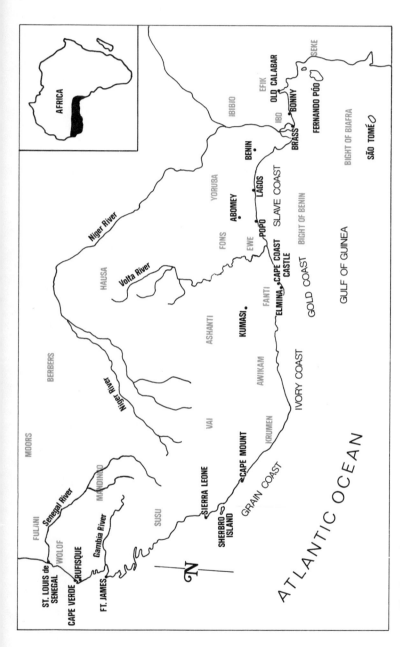

The Guinea Coast of West Africa in the 18th century. The names given by European traders to the various coastal regions—Grain Coast, Ivory Coast, Gold Coast—referred to the principal commodities available in these areas. The bights (bays) of Benin and Biafra were familiar landmarks to slavers navigating the Guinea Coast. Names of native tribes and peoples who lived in West Africa are shown on the map in gray.

2

The African Slave Trade

We must now turn to the modern era of slavery during which people from Africa were transported to the Americas, the West Indies, and the Arab world and forced to work for Arab and European slave owners. It was this period of slavery that made the black man's color a symbol of inequality which remains with him to this day in predominantly white societies.

Black Africans had been enslaved before the modern African slave trade began in the 15th century. Arabs and Turks had made slaves of peoples from various parts of the continent for centuries. (The modern conflict between the northern part of the Republic of Sudan and the southern portion is due partly to the fact that in the past the Arabs raided the south for Negro slaves.) In the black African states and empires of the Middle and Modern Ages, slavery was an accepted institution. African masters made use of domestic slaves and slaves who did hard manual labor on farms. But there is no evidence of plantation slavery, at least in sub-Saharan Africa, until Europeans came on the scene.

In the African states slaves were usually acquired in wars and raids; some people also sold themselves into slavery to pay their debts. The lot of slaves in most early African societies was not as hard as it became during the period of the slave trade. Household slaves were often considered members of the family, and there were cases in which a slave became a ruler after the death of all the important male members of the ruling house. This was possible because there was no color problem to complicate matters. But some favorite slaves of a king—his wives, for instance—were often sacrificed after his death.

With the entry of Europeans into the equatorial portions of Africa, things changed for the worse. The first Europeans to engage in the slave trade were the Portuguese, whose king took the title "Lord of Guinea" around 1480. Portuguese forts were established on the Guinea Coast of West Africa during this period, and slave markets in Lisbon sold black slaves to European buyers. The modern African slave trade had begun.

The new European market for slaves led native Africans to devise various means of acquiring captives among their own people to sell in return for rum, gin, brandy, firearms, and other foreign goods. The arms were used in the wars which took place all over West Africa in areas where the European influence was felt. Brutality increased, and the captives of the African wars were sold to European slave traders. Sometimes there were slave-raiding expe-

A standing saltcellar carved in ivory by the skilled African artists of Benin. Portuguese soldiers stand at attention around the bottom of the container. The figure on the top represents a European sailor peering from the crow's nest of his ship. Benin, a powerful native state located in present-day Nigeria, was at the height of its development in the late 15th century, when the Portuguese first came to the Guinea Coast.

Cape Coast Castle, on the Gold Coast. Built by the British in 1662, this fort was the headquarters of the Royal African Company in West Africa.

ditions during which villages were burned and the inhabitants rounded up and marched down to the coast to be sold. The slave trade made life in West Africa very insecure; it caused great devastation and seriously decreased the population.

Kidnapping was another source of supply for slaves and though some Africans indulged in it, it was practised most often by Europeans in the coastal areas. In certain parts of West Africa the natives forbade Europeans to catch slaves themselves; any white man indulging in the practice could be captured and enslaved. Europeans were never allowed to engage in slave raids upcountry, since that was a monopoly of Africans.

For over a hundred years the Portuguese controlled the slave trade, and during that period they invented or adapted words which became a part of the slavers' vocabulary. For example, the word *palaver*, meaning "a long parley or conference," is derived from the Portuguese word for "speech," *palavra*. Originally it referred to talks or negotiations between the slave traders and the African leaders. *Pickaninny*, a name for a little black child, is from the Portuguese *pequenino,* meaning "very little."

The Portuguese monopoly of the African slave trade ended with the 16th century. Portugal was united with Spain in 1580, and from that period on, other European powers challenged the Portuguese domination of the trade. By the end of the 17th century, Holland, England, France, and Denmark had joined the ranks of slaving nations. During the next century these nations competed for the human cargo which provided muscle power for the economies of the developing lands in the New World.

On the eastern coast of Africa and in the Sudan, Arab raiders started enslaving Negroes in the period of Islam's empire building, around the eighth century A.D. The main difference between the methods of the Arabs and those of most of the European traders was that the Arabs themselves actually went on slave-raiding expeditions and herded slaves to the coast. They also made permanent settlements on the east coast and on the island of Zanzibar, from which they controlled the slave traffic of the area. In the modern era the Arab slave trade became closely associated with the profitable trade in African ivory.

African States and the Slave Trade

Some students of the history of slavery seem to believe that the African slave trade was solely the work of European slavers who entered Africa and captured thousands of natives for transportation to Europe and the New World. As we have suggested in the preceding section, the evidence against this view is overwhelming. Native Africans played an important role in the buying and selling of black people.

During most of the slave trade period, the Guinea Coast of West Africa was dominated by several native kingdoms and states which had trading relations with the European nations. It was normal for Europeans engaged in the

The Gold Coast, about 1700. As the drawing indicates, the various forts in this area were very close together, often within sight of each other.

slave trade to secure land on the coast from the local king or chieftain, to be used as a site for a fort and trading center. The African leaders usually issued contracts called "notes" for the land and charged an annual rent for its use. The rented land on which the forts were built was the only legitimate area of operation for the European slavers. Since all trade had to be confined to the district of the fort, the custom was established whereby Africans went into the interior of their countries to bring slaves down to the coast.

From the beginning there was fierce competition among the European nations engaged in the slave trade along the coast of West Africa. The African chiefs often took sides in the battles between rival European powers holding forts in African territory, and it was normal for the side which did not have a chief's support to lose its fort to its opponents. Sometimes the Africans captured a fort, drove out the European governor, and put one of their own warriors in his place.

The only European colony established in West Africa during the slave trade period was the Portuguese settlement of Angola. All other attempts to extend the range of European control were unsuccessful. In most of their encounters with Africans, the European invaders were severely beaten and driven from the disputed territory. This happened quite often in the Gold Coast (modern Ghana). The Dutch, for instance, were defeated at Elmina in 1637, when they attempted to conquer the Fantes who inhabited the area near the fort. It was not until the later part of the 19th century that large-scale colonization became possible. Before that time Europeans found the Africans to be independent-minded and skilled at playing one slave-trading nation against another.

The African kings always stood on their dignity when dealing with the Europeans. A Dutch observer reported that at Anomabo in the Gold Coast English traders dared not contradict the local kings and had to obey their orders, which often included confinement within the walls of their forts. Ships which entered African ports had to fire salutes as a mark of respect to the local king; failure to do so could lead to a heavy fine.

All the accounts of the period clearly show that the Africans exhibited no feeling of inferiority in their relationships with the Europeans. In fact, many of the slave traders were impressed by the arrogance and craftiness of the natives with whom they dealt. The Africans seemed to have enjoyed outwitting the European traders. When trading in gold, for example, the white merchants often found that the Africans had given them brass filings instead of gold dust. This treachery was sometimes matched by the Europeans, who would invite African traders aboard their ships and then sail away with them as slaves. Occasionally the slavers also kidnapped "pawns"—people left with them as security during trading negotiations.

Throughout its history, the slave trade was a source of treachery and violence among both Europeans and Africans. In order to supply slaves for the European traders, the African kings usually found it necessary to attack neighboring kingdoms or weak tribes in the interior. In those battles the most powerful and largest kingdoms always won. Thus Ashanti, a large, warlike state in the Gold Coast, controlled the slave trade from the interior of that region. Dahomey was another powerful kingdom active in the trade. It had a proud ruler and an army of women whom the Europeans called Amazons. The king of Dahomey considered it condescension to shake hands with white men, but he was willing to condescend to the extent of supplying the European traders with slaves.

Most of the slaves supplied by the African traders were victims of wars and raids, but some were criminals or people who had sold themselves for debts. A man caught in adultery might also be sold into slavery. In return for depopulating their countries, the African kings obtained rum, guns, gunpowder, and trade goods from the Europeans. Rum was one of the most popular articles of trade on the Guinea Coast; Africans often refused to do business with American and West Indian traders who could not offer barrels of rum in exchange for slaves.

Negotiations between European and African slave traders at a Danish fort on the Gold Coast, late 18th century. Piled on the ground beside the negotiating parties are the guns and barrels of rum which the Europeans are offering in exchange for slaves.

So the Africans sold their brothers to work on the white man's sugar plantations, producing the ingredients for the rum which would buy more black slaves. And the tragic chain of events did not end here. As we have seen, the slave trade probably could not have flourished without the aid of Africans. Yet because of its success, black people from that time on have suffered under the burden of supposed inferiority that the slave trade imposed on them. Perhaps the lesson taught by the Greek tragedies has become reality for both blacks and whites: the sins of the fathers are being paid for by their descendants.

17th-Century Slave Trade—
England and the English Colonies in North America

Before continuing the story of the European nations which engaged in the African slave trade, it might be useful to consider the general question of slavery and serfdom in Europe itself during the slave trade period. Slavery still existed in 17th-century Europe. The majority of white slaves were prisoners of war, but some were people who had been sold for debts. Indentured laborers sent to the colonies to work on plantations served under conditions which, as we shall see, were often similar to slavery. There were still serfs in some European countries, especially in Russia. Pirates roamed the seas from the Atlantic to the Mediterranean, making slaves of men of every nationality.

The 17th century as a whole was a harsh and brutal period in human history. Men of this era often treated each other like animals, though they found time on Sundays and holy days to listen to eloquent sermons on the saving of souls. Stealing was punished by death in most countries, and hunting on a nobleman's estate without permission was a capital offense. White convicts were deported to the colonies to work in slave gangs, and their treatment was as inhumane as that given to black slaves.

The African slave trade was the crowning brutality of a brutal age. During the 17th century, England took her place among the nations engaged in this cruel enterprise and rapidly came to dominate the trade as the Portuguese had done in the preceding century. In 1663 the English royal family entered the slave trade with the formation of the Company of Royal Adventurers of England Trading in Africa. The company, which was chartered under the Duke of York, the brother of King Charles II, branded its slaves with the letters DY to indicate their royal ownership. The king himself invested money in his brother's business venture and, to promote its success, he issued a new coin, the guinea, made of West African gold.

The Duke of York, later King James II, played a significant role in the development of the English slave trade during the 17th century.

As we have indicated, there was much rivalry among the European slave nations doing business in West Africa. During the last half of the 17th century, the Dutch managed to capture most of the forts that the English had built on the Guinea Coast. The Royal Adventurers and King Charles lost all their money as a result of these encounters. But in 1672 the English formed another company, the Royal African Company, again with Charles II as one of its investors, and started building more forts in West Africa.

Apart from these chartered companies, there were other English traders who were called "interlopers." They went anywhere and refused to recognize the official monopoly of the companies chartered by the Crown. To protect the Royal African Company, interloping was at first made a capital offense. When that failed to discourage the inter-

This guinea, struck in 1676, bears the image of Charles II and the badge of the Royal African Company on its obverse (front). The company badge, a small elephant which appears below the king's head, indicates that the coin is made of West African gold.

lopers, a 10 percent tax was imposed on all traders who chose to compete with the company. But in spite of this tax the Royal African Company did not earn enough to maintain its forts.

Most of the African slaves bought by the European traders in the 17th century were exported to the Americas and the West Indies. The first black slaves to enter what later became the United States were probably those imported in 1526 by a Spaniard, Lucas Vásquez de Ayllon, who had attempted to found a colony in the Virginia area. (The attempt failed.) There were Negro slaves in Mexico and Brazil in the 1530s, and the Spanish brought slaves to Florida in 1565.

The slave trade to the English colonies of North America began in 1619, when a Dutch ship landed 20 Negroes in Jamestown. However, trade in African slaves did not become immediately successful because of the availability of white indentured servants in the New World. Indentured servants were people bound by contract to work for a certain number of years. During most of the 17th century

Landing of the first black slaves in the British colonies of North America, Jamestown, 1619.

they provided a cheaper form of labor than the purchase of black slaves could supply.

Many of the indentured servants brought to the English colonies had agreed to sell their labor as a means of paying for their passage to the New World, but others had been kidnapped and forced into bondage, or deported.

Kidnapping of children was common in England during this period, as was the deporting of convicted criminals, who were often considered slaves and bound to service for life. Victims of war could also be enslaved: during the 17th century several groups of Scottish captives and rebellious Englishmen were sold in the American colonies and the West Indies. (The English king always made a commission on the sale of such prisoners.) At times religious persecution made possible the enslavement of children. In 1659, for example, the children of Quakers living in the New England colonies were sold to planters in Virginia and Barbados.

It is recorded that the conditions under which the indentured servants traveled to the colonies were worse than those the black slaves experienced. African slaves were regarded as more valuable cargo than the white workers, so they were often given better care during the voyage. As a result of their treatment, thousands of indentured servants died before they reached America.

The trade in white indentured servants continued into the 18th century, but in the 17th century it took precedence over the Negro slave trade in the North American colonies. Even when African slaves became more common in the colonies, the question of race did not enter into the slave trade at first. Negroes, who were frequently referred to as servants, were enslaved for a fixed term, after which they were freed and given some land, as was done with white indentured servants. As comrades in affliction, white and black servants often ran away together. They were also sold together and intermarriage was not unknown.

The issue of race, however, was gradually introduced into colonial slavery as the impracticality of the indenture system became increasingly apparent. The fact that indentured servants were bound only to temporary servitude meant that the colonial labor force had to be constantly renewed. Problems were also created by the fact that masters and servants in the English colonies were so much alike in race, faith, and social background. Masters found it difficult to maintain absolute control over their white indentured servants, who were Christians and often Englishmen as well. This common background and appearance also made identifying and recapturing runaway servants difficult. Lastly, the enslaving of fellow Christians for long periods of time raised troublesome questions of conscience.

But Negro slavery presented none of these problems. Africans were members of an alien, presumably inferior, race. They had their black skins for identification and they were heathens, so one could keep them in bondage forever without suffering any pangs of conscience.

Virginia was the first colony to legally establish the distinction between white and black servants. In 1662 the Virginia assembly ruled that all Negro slaves should become "perpetual servants." Two years later Maryland ruled that all Negroes should be considered slaves and forbade racial intermarriage. In 1667 Virginia decreed that baptism could not confer freedom on black slaves. Maryland passed a similar law in 1671.

It seems obvious that the seeds of America's later racial problems were sown in the colonial period. During those years the inferior position of the black man was firmly established by law and convention, and black people were officially deprived of that dignity which is normally associated with human beings.

The Slave's Journey to the New World

The busiest period of the slave trade was the 18th century. By then the European traders had established well-defined relationships with the African countries from which slaves were exported. All they had to do was to devise better methods of winning bigger profits from the traffic in human beings. The question of morality had not arisen.

The journey of the typical slave from the forests and hills of Africa to the plantations of the West Indies and the Americas was extremely dangerous. It began in violence and confusion when the African slavers raided the up-country villages and captured men, women, and children to be sold on the coast. The slavers moved their captives in coffles, the term used for a train of slaves or animals driven along together. Members of the coffle were generally tied by the neck to poles which they pulled along; the slave driver walked beside them and whipped those who grew tired and slowed down. Many of the captives died of fatigue or disease, and only a small proportion ever reached the coast. Those who could make the journey without breaking down were sold to European factors, merchants dealing in slaves, who were usually employed by the trading companies. The factors stored the slaves in cells in the forts along the coast to await transportation to the colonies. (Some of these cells can still be seen in the Castle at Elmina in Ghana.)

The voyage across the Atlantic was the most dangerous part of the journey to the New World. The bewildered slaves, most of whom had never seen the ocean before, were packed like sardines in the small European ships. If the weather was fair during the voyage, the captives were allowed to spend the day chained on deck; here they were

Slaves being transported to a Portuguese ship. Since there were few good harbors on the Guinea Coast, large canoes were used to ferry the slaves to the European ships anchored offshore. The canoes were often manned by the Krumen, a sea-going tribe skilled in navigating the turbulent Guinea Coast surf.

often forced to "dance" for exercise while someone used a whip to make them more active. They were given meager meals and sent down to the holds in the evening. In bad weather slaves were kept in the crowded holds day and night.

The hold of a slave ship, usually about five feet high, often had a kind of shelf or platform built around its walls, which increased the vessel's cargo space. Both the shelf and the area below it were filled with slaves chained together and often packed in so tightly that they could sleep lying only on their sides. Women and children were kept in

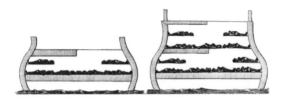

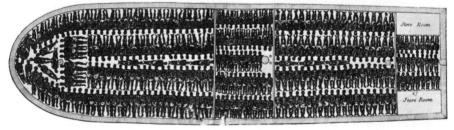

Diagram of a slave ship, showing the way in which slaves were packed into the holds. The shelf or platform used to increase available space can be seen clearly in the cross-section drawing.

a different part of the ship and treated more leniently than the men. The conditions below deck were such that many died of suffocation. Sanitary provisions were almost nonexistent and infectious diseases of various kinds were common. In case of epidemics, slaves who were infected were simply thrown overboard to prevent the disease from spreading.

It is hardly surprising that the slaves disliked being herded like beasts on board the European slave ships. Many Africans actually believed that their white captors were cannibals and were going to eat them. To escape this fate, some committed suicide during the voyage by jumping overboard, refusing food, or knocking their heads against the rails. The voyage itself killed many slaves. In general, conditions on the ships were so bad that only the strongest could survive the long journey over the Atlantic; it has been estimated that the average slave ship lost 13 percent of its cargo during the crossing. The slavers did their best to keep most of their captives alive, however, since there could be no profit in a dead cargo. Because long voyages increased the death rate among the slaves, the ship captains always tried to shorten their routes. Depending on the route taken and the weather encountered, the journey across the Atlantic—the so-called Middle Passage—could take anywhere from three weeks to three months.

There was always the danger of mutiny among the slaves on board the ships. To prevent rebellion, the captives were kept in chains while in the holds and watched by guards with guns while on deck. It was found that when Africans of the same tribe traveled together they could mutiny more easily, since they understood each other's language. Therefore efforts were made to mix the tribes on

This dramatic painting by the English artist J. W. M. Turner pictures slaves who have been thrown overboard still bound in chains. Slave ships often carried insurance against the necessity of "jettisoning" their cargo. Thus slaves who might not survive the voyage were sometimes thrown overboard so that the insurance could be collected.

each ship. Very often the warlike blacks, especially those from the Gold Coast, who despised other more docile Africans, were put in charge of the slaves to keep them in order. Human beings are such that their oppressors can easily use them to oppress someone else. It gives the persecuted a needed sense of power and importance to be able to dominate others as they themselves are dominated. No wonder freed slaves often kept slaves of their own.

Slaves on the deck of a slave ship. Their emaciated condition was common to most Africans who managed to survive the rigors of the Middle Passage.

In spite of the precautions, there were many mutinies which usually proved costly to the slave traders. Apart from mutinies, the slavers also had to fight against the hostility of the natives along the coast. In the 18th century the European factors and their crews did more kidnapping than they had previously. In retaliation, the natives sometimes "cut off" (captured) the ships and took away the slaves to be sold to other traders. On the whole, it can be said that the Africans did not accept their fate passively, and that the Europeans got as much as they gave. Life for both the slave and the slaver was dangerous, and the craftier person won the day.

In addition to the dangers of mutinies and attacks by natives along the African coasts, the slave ships were also threatened by privateers. These were armed ships of foreign nations roaming the seas in search of vessels carrying merchandise and slaves. Privateering generally occurred during the few days before the slave ships landed in the West Indies.

When the slaves reached their destination, they were sold in various ways. Sometimes an entire shipload of captives was purchased by a single planter or group of planters. Generally, however, a factor took charge of retailing slaves for a profit. On occasion, the ship captains themselves did the selling by parading the slaves through the streets of the town. An observer who had witnessed one of these parades described its members as "walking skeletons covered over with a piece of tanned leather, . . . a resurrection of skin and bones . . . risen from the grave or escaped from Surgeon's Hall."

The most common method of sale was a combination of the public auction and the "scramble." The sick and disabled slaves were first taken from the ships and sold by auction. They generally brought half the price of healthy Negroes, but sometimes a slave in damaged condition could be bought for as little as one dollar. The traders often attempted to hide diseases among their merchandise, and some seemingly healthy slaves died soon after purchase.

Selling by the "scramble" meant paying a standard

price for any man, woman, boy, or girl on the ship. After the prices had been agreed upon, a gun was fired and the purchasers scrambled on board to make their choices. The Africans were terrified by these wild assaults because they thought that the white cannibals were preparing to eat them! It was at such times that many slaves decided to run away or commit suicide.

Advertisement from a Charleston newspaper in 1766, announcing the sale of a cargo of slaves from the Windward Coast.

TO BE SOLD. on board the Ship *Bance-Island*, on tuesday the 6th of *May* next, at *Ashley-Ferry*; a choice cargo of about 250 fine healthy

NEGROES,

just arrived from the Windward & Rice Coast. —The utmost care has already been taken, and shall be continued, to keep them free from the least danger of being infected with the SMALL-POX, no boat having been on board, and all other communication with people from *Charles-Town* prevented.

Austin, Laurens, & Appleby.

N. B. Full one Half of the above Negroes have had the SMALL-POX in their own Country.

3

Slavery in the European Colonies of the New World

The modern African slave trade was able to exist and to flourish because the institution of slavery existed and flourished in some parts of the contemporary world. By the 17th century, slavery had become an important element in the developing economies of many European colonies in the New World. This was particularly true in the islands of the West Indies and in parts of South America. In these regions several European nations—Portugal, Spain, England, France, the Netherlands, Denmark—had established colonies which in varying degrees made use of slave labor. In order to understand the real inhumanity of the slave trade as well as the difficulties faced by those who wished to end it, it is necessary to know something about the slave's position in these colonial societies.

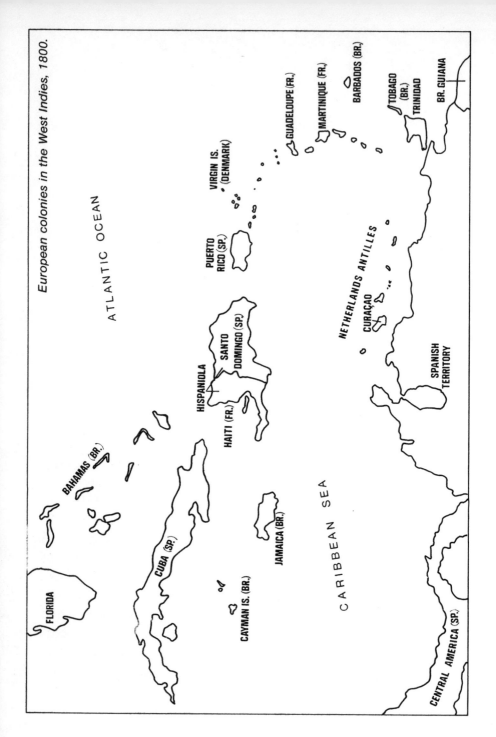

European colonies in the West Indies, 1800.

ATLANTIC OCEAN

BAHAMAS (BR.)

FLORIDA

CUBA (SP.)

CAYMAN IS. (BR.)

JAMAICA (BR.)

HISPANIOLA

HAITI (FR.)

SANTO DOMINGO (SP.)

PUERTO RICO (SP.)

VIRGIN IS. (DENMARK)

GUADELOUPE (FR.)

MARTINIQUE (FR.)

BARBADOS (BR.)

TOBAGO (BR.)

TRINIDAD

BR. GUIANA

NETHERLANDS ANTILLES

CURAÇAO

SPANISH TERRITORY

CARIBBEAN SEA

CENTRAL AMERICA (SP.)

Brazil

Slavery was an important institution in Brazil, the large Portuguese colony on the South American mainland. As we have noted, Portugal was the first European nation to engage in the African slave trade. In the 15th century the Portuguese not only sold slaves on the world market but also brought African captives into Portugal itself to work on the land. The nation's inhabitants thus developed a tradition of slave holding and a familiarity with black people which affected the establishment of slavery in Portugal's American colony during the 16th century. Portugal was the only European colonial power to have had this kind of preparation for the slave-owning experience of the New World.

Another aspect of Portugal's history which may have influenced the development of Portuguese slavery in Brazil was the Moorish domination of the mother country during the medieval period. In the eighth century A.D. Moors from North Africa invaded the Iberian Peninsula and established powerful Muslim kingdoms which ruled Portugal and large parts of Spain for almost 500 years. The Moors, of course, were not black Africans but Arabs and Berbers, dark-skinned Caucasian peoples who possessed a highly developed culture. Portugal's close contact with this sophisticated, non-European civilization and the genetic mixing of the two ethnic groups helped to shape the racial attitudes and ideals of the Portuguese nation. (Since the Spanish people were also dominated by the Moors for a long period of time, they were probably influenced in a similar manner.)

All of these factors undoubtedly had some influence on the system of slavery which grew up in colonial Brazil. In

A 17th-century Brazilian sugar mill. In the early years of Brazil's colonial history most African slaves worked on large plantations, growing, cutting, and processing sugarcane.

the 16th and 17th centuries, sugar was the important crop in the Portuguese colony, and African slave labor was used extensively on the many sugar plantations in northeastern Brazil. Brazilian sugar estates in the colonial period were usually quite large and separated from each other by great distances. They were very much like small feudal kingdoms ruled over by the sugar planter, the "lord of the plantation," who had under his control a large group of people, most of whom were slaves. The planter worked his slaves hard and sometimes treated them cruelly, but there often existed a close relationship of mutual dependence between the white master and his black workers. In the isolation of Brazil's tropical wilderness, the planter was the governor and protector of his people, as well as their taskmaster. He saw to it that they had food, clothing, shelter, and religious guidance. (All Brazilian slaves had to be baptized and were considered full-fledged members of the Catholic Church.)

Under the Brazilian plantation system, the master depended on his slaves for many services in addition to their labor in the sugar fields. Most of the white children who grew up in the plantation Big House had a black nurse, often considered an honored member of the family, who nursed them as infants and helped to raise them. Other household slaves also had personal relationships with their white masters and mistresses, since the isolation of the Brazilian sugar estate usually led the planter and his family to seek companionship among the black people with whom they lived so closely. Often the relationship between master and slave was sexual in nature; the black concubine and her mulatto children were familiar features of the plantation Big House throughout much of Brazilian colonial history. In the colony's early days relatively few Portuguese women came to settle in the New World, and unions between white men and black slave women became quite common. This tradition of racial mixing continued, and, as a result, the population of the colony soon came to include a large number of people with varying degrees of mixed blood. Eventually, this mulatto group became more numerous than those Brazilians of unmixed racial ancestry, either white or black.

In the colonial period many Brazilians of African descent, blacks as well as people of mixed blood, were not enslaved but free. Like the Spanish colonies, Brazil provided numerous opportunities for the slave to obtain his freedom; voluntary manumission by the master was a custom approved and encouraged by both church and society, and the slave could also arrange to purchase his own freedom. Free Negroes and mulattoes occupied many different social and economic positions in Brazilian colonial society. Most were laborers, tradesmen, or artisans, but some eventually became wealthy and powerful. White skin was more favored than black in the Brazilian racial system, but, as an old Brazilian folk saying ironically explains, "Money whitens the skin." Portuguese experience in the Old World had made it easier for the Portuguese colonists to view racial

A slave market in Rio de Janeiro, early 19th century.

differences as only one of the factors that separated people into social groups.

Brazil ceased to be a colony in 1822, when she declared her independence from Portugal. During the last part of the colonial period and the first years of independence, treatment of Negro slaves in Brazil changed for the worse. The importance of sugar declined during this period and coffee growing gradually came to dominate the country's economy. The coffee planters of the south were men with interests and goals different from those of their colonial predecessors, the lords of the northern sugar estates. The coffee plantations in the São Paulo area were not so much feudal estates as agricultural enterprises designed to produce a profit. Thus the relationship of the planter to his slaves was primarily economic, lacking in the sense of paternal responsibility which often bound the northern planter to his slaves. Under such conditions, Brazilian slavery became more harsh. However, since this development took place not too many years prior to the abolition of of slavery in the late 19th century, it did not do irreparable damage to relations between the races in Brazil. The traditional attitudes and social relationships survived and helped to make the transition from slavery to freedom relatively easy for both the freed slaves and the society into which they were absorbed.

The Spanish Colonies

Spain had one of the largest colonial empires in the New World; in the 16th century her holdings included Mexico, Central America, large portions of South America, and several islands in the West Indies, the most important of which was Cuba. Negro slavery existed to some extent in all the Spanish possessions, but it was most highly developed and most significant in the island colonies of the West Indies.

Spain began to use Negro slaves in her West Indian colonies early in the 16th century. The colonists had originally attempted to enslave the native Indians of the islands but had found them unable to cope with the work on the land. When an influential clergyman, Bartolomé de las Casas, saw the devastation of the Indian population caused by Spanish oppression, he urged King Charles I to bring African laborers to the island. Las Casas almost immediately

The Spanish priest Bartolomé de las Casas was called the Apostle of the Indies because of his efforts to protect the native Indians of the islands. His concern for their welfare led him to advocate the use of African slaves in the Spanish colonies.

This 17th-century print shows the Indians of Hispaniola enslaved by Spanish colonists.

regretted his suggestion but it had already borne fruit. In 1517 the king arranged to have 4,000 Negroes transported to the colonies by the slave merchants of Genoa. The Spanish colonists would be allowed to buy black slaves imported by others, but they could not go to Africa to obtain slaves themselves. This custom was formalized through the so-called *asiento*, a contract between Spain and another country or a trading company for supplying slaves to the Spanish colonies. For many years the slave-trading powers of the New World fought each other for the privilege of holding the profitable Spanish *asiento*.

At first Negroes in the Spanish colonies were treated as badly as the Indians had been, but eventually laws were passed to improve their condition. These laws were sometimes ignored and offenses against them went unpunished, but their very existence indicates that Spanish attitudes toward slaves differed from those of most of the European colonists in the New World.

Spanish masters were required to prepare their slaves for baptism within a year of their importation, and to send them to mass on Sundays and festivals. They were bound by law to allow a slave to choose a wife from any district on the island. If the woman chosen belonged to a distant estate, either the man's or the woman's master had to purchase the other slave so that the pair could marry and live together. Married couples could not be separated by sale, and families could not be broken up by sale for the master's debts. Although legally slaves could not own property, Spanish custom allowed them to own houses, land, and even other slaves.

The most distinctive feature of Spanish slavery was the opportunity it provided for the slave to obtain his freedom. There were two types of slaves in the Spanish system—those who could be sold for any sum by their owners, and others, known as *coartados*, whose price had been limited or "cut." A slave could buy his own freedom by offering to his master a sum of money equivalent to his market value. Or he could pay part of this amount and thus make himself a *coartado*; that is, the partial sum he had paid would be subtracted from the total price required for his freedom. Then he could continue to make payments in installments of not less than $50, until he had paid the whole purchase price. A slave who had become a *coartado* and was attempting to buy his freedom was usually allowed to hire himself out as a worker, providing that he paid his master a part of the money he earned.

Spanish slaves could negotiate their own freedom or they could obtain the aid of a local magistrate, the Protector of Slaves. If a master would not accept the sum offered by a slave, the matter was referred to the Protector, who would settle the dispute by arbitration. The maximum price which an owner could demand for a slave's liberty was $300. If a Spanish slave were ill-treated by his master, he could get the Protector to grant him a license to be resold. The owner was then obliged to sell him to any willing purchaser.

Slavery was not always hereditary under the Spanish system. Children born of slave parents did not automatically become slaves but could be freed for a fee either before or immediately after birth. Moreover, the voluntary freeing of slaves was a practice encouraged by both church and society.

Those who gained most from the Spanish system were the town slaves and household slaves, who had marketable skills. During the 16th and 17th centuries, many of the Negroes in Cuba, Spain's most important West Indian colony, worked in urban areas and had skilled occupations. Cuban slaves were craftsmen and tradesmen, construction workers and small farmers. They often operated with little supervision and had some free time to devote to their own interests. Thus they were frequently able to earn the money to pay for their freedom. In the 18th and 19th centuries, when plantation crops like sugar came to dominate the island's economy, the position of the average Cuban slave changed for the worse. The cultivation of sugar demanded

A sugarcane field in modern Cuba. Today many West Indians, the descendants of slaves, work in the sugar fields as did their ancestors.

long hours of unpleasant work; the numerous slaves employed on the plantations were treated more harshly and had less freedom than those engaged in other occupations. However, even the plantation slaves could make a little money by selling some of the food which they were permitted to grow for their own use.

There is convincing evidence that slaves in the Spanish territories took full advantage of the opportunities to gain their freedom. In 1817 there were only 199,000 slaves in Cuba out of a colored population of 383,000. When the former Spanish colony of Trinidad was ceded to Great Britain in 1802, it had 21,000 slaves and 14,000 free people of color. Free blacks had, in theory at least, all the rights and privileges of free whites. There may have been abuses, but in general it is fair to say that the Spaniards made the path to freedom relatively smooth. They did not consider the slave's color a sign of necessary inferiority. People of mixed black and white ancestry became very common in the Spanish West Indies.

The British West Indies

Great Britain was another European power with colonial possessions in the West Indies. During the 18th century the plantation economies of many of the British islands depended on the extensive use of Negro slaves. The system of slavery existing in the British West Indies was different in many ways from slavery in the Spanish and Portuguese colonies. British slaves did not have a legal right to purchase their own freedom. Freedom depended solely on the wishes of the slave owner, who might or might not agree to grant it. Often the price fixed by the master was exorbitant. For instance, in 1824 the market value of a slave in Jamaica was £45 sterling (equivalent to about $126, in today's money), but slaves often had to pay between £100 and £200 sterling to free themselves. As a result, the only slaves who could usually afford to buy their freedom were craftsmen and skilled workers. In some British colonies, masters who wanted to free their slaves had to obtain the governor's consent and also pay a heavy tax for the privilege.

The aim of all the British restrictions on freeing slaves was to limit the number of free black people in the colonies. The policy was very successful: in 1827, there were 20,000 more free Negroes in Cuba alone than in all of the British West Indies.

In the British colonies it was generally assumed that any person who was a Negro was also a slave. If a black man without a master could not produce evidence of his free status, he could be advertised for sale. Even if he were born of free parents in one colony, he could be enslaved elsewhere. Skin color was considered an indelible mark of enslavement.

The harbor of Bridgetown on the island of Barbados, late 17th century. Settled by the British in 1627, Barbados was one of the most prosperous sugar-producing colonies in the West Indies.

British slaves, unlike Spanish slaves, had no personal legal status. As the abolitionist William Wilberforce said, "In contemplation of the law they are not persons but mere chattels." It was only in the 1820s that the murder of Negroes in the British colonies was made a capital offense. British slaves could not be legally married. They could not give evidence in court against free men, whether black or white, presumably because they were not able to distinguish between truth and falsehood.

As we have seen, Spanish slaves were usually baptized soon after their arrival in the West Indies. However, no provisions were made for the religious conversion of British

slaves. The established Church of England in the colonies catered to whites only. The British statesman George Canning expressed the common belief of his day when he said that the Church of England "was no more calculated for the negro than for the brute animal who shares his toil." The task of converting black slaves became the duty of dissenting sects like the Methodists and Moravians. Their activities in the colonies were suspect, and their ministers were often threatened by members of the established church.

Because of the harsh treatment given to their slaves, the British colonies had more slave rebellions than the Spanish ever had. The main aim of the British planters was to make money, and any means that could help them to

A 19th-century sugar-boiling house. Juice squeezed from the sugarcane had to be heated in order to produce raw sugar. The process of making sugar without the aid of modern machinery was hard and exacting work.

achieve this end was acceptable. The money-making crop on Jamaica, Barbados, and most of the other British-owned islands was sugar. Sugar plantations were usually worked by gangs of slaves grouped according to age. The first gang, called the "great" gang, consisted of men and women aged from 16 to 50, who did the heavy field work. The gang's Negro leader was known as the head driver; he had a crook as the emblem of his authority and a whip to urge the slaves to work hard. The second gang was made up of men and women over 50, and boys and girls from 12 to 16, who had lighter tasks to perform. The "small" gang consisted of children of 6 to 12 years, who weeded the fields under the supervision of a woman driver. Old women did the cooking or looked after the youngest children, and old men were employed as watchmen.

In addition to the gangs owned by the master of the

estate, there were other slaves, called jobbers, who could be hired on a temporary basis. They were the property of a contractor and could work as a relief team for any planter. The work of the jobbers was hard and they often lived under unwholesome conditions, since their temporary employers were not concerned about their general welfare.

Slaves normally worked very long hours on the sugar plantations. During the crop season, when the sugarcane was cut and processed, they often labored in shifts throughout the night. Since it was felt that the whip was a spur to good work, slave drivers used it frequently to brutalize their fellow human beings. Because of their harsh treatment and the unhealthy conditions under which they lived, plantation slaves often developed diseases that destroyed their health and cut short their lives.

Sugar was the major crop in the British West Indies, but the islands also produced cotton and coffee on a much smaller scale. Slavery on these estates was considered easier and less unhealthy than that on the sugar plantations. We have little information about the condition of slaves on the grazing estates where cattle were raised.

For many years in the British West Indies, a master's power over a slave was absolute. If a slave were killed in the course of punishment, his owner was not even fined for the crime. In 1822, a government commission was appointed to investigate the administration of justice in the British colonies. One of the commissioners reported that "no man or set of men has legal power to call [the slave master] to account for working his slave as long as he likes, for whipping him as much as he pleases, for chaining, for starving him." Such was the Christian treatment that black people received in the British colonies.

Other European Colonies in the West Indies

The French colonies in the West Indies had a set of laws similar to the Spanish regulations governing the status and treatment of slaves. However, the French laws, called the *Code Noir*, were useless since they merely advised masters against mistreating slaves but did not guarantee them adequate protection. The *Code Noir* declared slaves "incapable of possessing anything except to the use of their masters," or of receiving any gift or inheritance. They could be brought to court only as criminals or witnesses, and their evidence did not carry much weight. Slaves were included in their masters' personal estates and could be disposed of like other movable property; however, slaves between the ages of 14 and 60 could not be sold apart from the plantation in payment of the master's debts. (This law was intended to insure the slave a permanent place to live.) Further, a family belonging to the same owner could not be sold separately.

Although French masters could punish slaves at their own discretion, they were not permitted to torture, maim, or kill them. Slaves could not marry without their masters' consent. They were to be baptized and educated in the Catholic faith to improve their condition and allowed a full day's rest on Sundays and religious festivals. The master also had to provide them with food and clothing. When ill-treated, slaves could complain to a magistrate.

French slave owners usually ignored the provisions of these laws. The primary aim of the planters was economic gain, and the law was not allowed to interfere in their enterprises. A French officer who visited the colony of Saint-Domingue in 1751 reported that some planters overworked their slaves and treated those who were old or sick worse than their dogs and horses. Slaves sent to prison had to be examined by a doctor since some masters would make false charges against slaves who were ill in order to avoid medical expenses. Such mistreatment almost always went unpunished since the French slave was completely at the mercy of his master. An observer described the legal system in the French colonies as divided into two independent jurisdictions: public regulations like the *Code Noir*, and the private rules and customs by which the colonists actually lived. Since the public laws were ineffective, the planters in the colonies sometimes elected local committees to deal with matters affecting slaves and to hear complaints. However, the justice given by such committees was unimpressive.

The French colonists, unlike many of the English planters, lived permanently in the islands. They regarded the West Indies as their home and tried to maintain the same kind of racial separation there as would have existed in France. The French did not approve of any form of open sexual relationship between whites and blacks. On the island of St. Lucia, persons of color were forbidden by law to wear the same kind of clothes as white people. They could not be referred to in any legal document as "Mr." or "Madam" but merely as "that man" and "that woman." However, the French were more generous in granting slaves their freedom than the British were. They also imported a larger proportion of female slaves to enable the men to obtain partners, though they did not care much whether slaves married or not.

The Danes controlled several islands in the West Indies and kept slaves on their sugar plantations. They had a savage code designed to frighten the slaves but were hu-

A slave market on the island of Martinique, early 19th century. The French colonies had laws regulating the treatment of slaves, but they were more often ignored than observed by French slave owners.

mane in their actual dealings with them. It was said that the Danish planters in the 18th century could sleep with their doors and windows open without any sense of insecurity. The Dutch, on the other hand, had a reputation for being hard taskmasters. Their laws on slavery were better than the British laws since they provided for a Protector, but they were effectively ignored. Dutch treatment of slaves was particularly harsh in the colony of Guiana, on the northeastern coast of South America. Here the Dutch settlers were in continual conflict with a group of fugitive slaves called maroons. There were pitched battles between the planters and maroons, and brutal executions took place when the rebellious slaves were subdued.

Dutch cruelty to slaves manifested itself in many ways. Once when a white man pleaded for a slave girl who had been suspended by her wrists and was being beaten, the overseer doubled the lashes; that was his way, he said, with slaves for whom people interceded. Sometimes Dutch slaves were flogged to death. They were also wantonly killed, and no charges could be brought against the murderers. Slaves who were unfit for work could be starved or secretly disposed of.

The Dutch employed their slaves on what is known as piecework. Each slave was expected to do a certain piece of work within a certain time, after which he was in theory free to work for himself. He was severely punished if he failed to complete his task. On the other hand, those who worked hard enough to finish ahead of time were usually not allowed to rest but were given harder work to do. The effectiveness of the piecework system was neutralized by this kind of cruelty.

Colonial North America

Slavery existed in the British colonies of North America as well as in the British islands of the West Indies. As we have already noted, during the earliest years of settlement in North America, white indentured servants made up the largest part of the colonial labor force. By the end of the 17th century, however, Negro slavery had gradually become the dominant labor system in several colonies. Growing numbers of black slaves were being imported from the West

Indigo was one of the commodities produced by slave labor in colonial North America. The process of extracting the blue dye from the indigo plant is illustrated in this 18th-century drawing of a South Carolina plantation.

Indies and Africa to work on the plantations of the South and, to a much lesser extent, in the towns and agricultural areas of the North.

The plantation crops in colonial North America were tobacco, rice, and indigo, a plant used to make a blue dye. Cotton, which later became the staple crop in much of the South, was grown only on a very small scale in the colonial era. During the 18th century, the large tobacco plantations of Virginia and Maryland and the rice and indigo plantations of the Carolinas employed many Negro slaves who did the toilsome work necessary to grow these crops. The cultivation of rice was particularly taxing and unpleasant, requiring long hours of labor in flooded fields, on plantations usually located in hot, malaria-ridden areas. White rice planters in the Carolinas spent as little time as possible on their estates, but black slaves were considered to be ideally suited for work under such unhealthy conditions.

As the slave populations grew in the various colonies, slave codes were developed to keep the blacks under control. The harshness of the codes generally varied in relation to the number of slaves in a given territory. In South Carolina, for example, blacks outnumbered whites by the beginning of the 18th century; the colony, accordingly, had a very stringent slave code patterned after those used in the British West Indies. Laws governing slaves in the northern colonies were relatively mild, since the white colonists in these areas had little to fear from the few Negroes living in their midst.

There were not many slaves living in the North during the 18th century, but the traffic in slaves was an important factor in the economy of the area. Many New England merchants, ship builders, and seamen made their fortunes

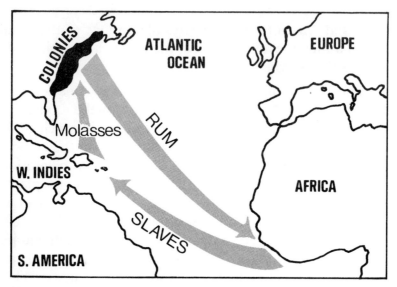

The route of the triangular trade linked the North American colonies, the Guinea Coast of West Africa, and the islands of the West Indies in an exchange of human lives for rum and molasses.

in the American slave trade. Thriving colonial cities such as Newport, Salem, and Boston owed much of their early prosperity to the notorious triangular trade, which carried rum to Africa, slaves to the islands of the West Indies, and molasses to the rum manufacturers of New England. Thus, although slavery itself did not take root in the northern colonies, the investments of northern merchants and the voyages of New England ship captains contributed to the institution's development in the New World.

The growth of slavery in North America, gradual and often unplanned, continued throughout the colonial period. By the late 18th century, when the colonies severed their ties with England, Negro slavery had become a significant part of the new nation's social and economic life.

4

Slavery in the Old World

The greatest demand for slaves during the modern era came from the European colonies in the New World, but there was also a thriving Old World market for slaves in Arab lands. We have mentioned that the Arabs were among the first non-Africans in history to enslave black people. For many years, beginning around the eighth century A.D., Arabs engaged in slaving throughout East Africa and the Sudan. The East African slave trade in the 18th and 19th centuries was closely connected with the trade in African ivory.

Arabs had colonized the east coast of Africa and the island of Zanzibar in the early medieval period, but in the 16th century the Portuguese challenged Arab control and took possession of most of the Arab-held territory. After 200 years of Portuguese domination, Arabs from Muscat, a small country on the southeastern tip of the Arabian Peninsula, recaptured Zanzibar and the territory on the coast. The traditional Arab trade in slaves and ivory was renewed; in the 19th century it reached its highest peak in profit and destruction.

The Arabs obtained their slaves and ivory by traveling on foot into the interior of East and Central Africa. They got as far as the Congo forests but traveled and settled primarily around the Great Lakes of East Africa—Victoria, Nyanza, and Tanganyika. Although they made no formal claim to the territory, the Arabs actually controlled most of this part of Africa until European colonization in the area.

Wherever the Arabs went, they burned down villages and kidnapped human beings who were forced to carry ivory to the coast. The ivory itself was usually taken, by force or sometimes by barter, from the abundant supply of elephant tusks out of which the natives made fences, tools, ornaments, and other everyday items. (Ivory had no special value for Africans.) Both the ivory and the captives who carried it were eventually sold in the great trading markets of Zanzibar. The many European and American merchants who were eager to purchase African ivory helped to keep the Arab traders in business.

Like so many of the other slave traders, the Arabs were very treacherous in their dealings with the Africans. They often made agreements with the native leaders only to break them. After accepting the hospitality of a chief they would murder him, sack his towns and villages, and take their inhabitants captive. The Arabs' guns and ammunition gave them a great advantage over the Africans. Also, their skin color—as strange to the blacks as Cortes's was to the Indians of Mexico—often helped to frighten their victims into submission.

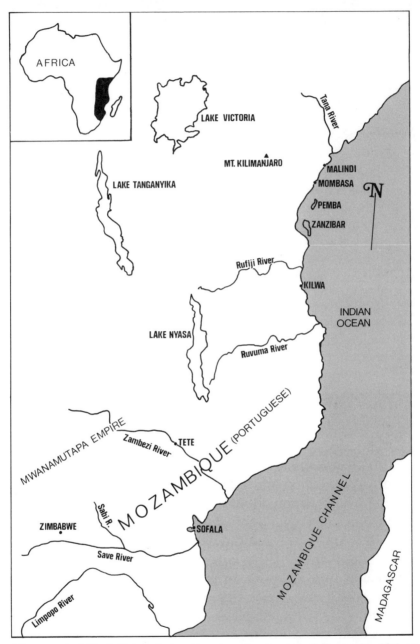

The coast of East Africa during the slave-trade period. From the 12th to the 15th centuries the Arab-dominated cities of Kilwa, Mombasa, Sofala, Malindi, and Zanzibar served as commercial centers for the thriving Indian Ocean trade. In the 16th century the Portuguese captured many of the coastal cities, and East African commerce declined. When it was revived in the 18th century by a new group of Arab settlers, slaves and ivory were the principal commodities of trade.

The Arabs who traded in slaves and ivory sent their cargoes to the coast in coffles. A passage from the book *Ivory, Scourge of Africa*, by E. D. Moore, gives a vivid description of the conditions under which Arab slaves traveled:

> The horror, the misery, the cruelty of the slave coffle never has been nor can be adequately pictured. Probably not more than one in five of the captive marchers, as authorities of the day have estimated, ever reached the ocean. Bowed down by the weight of fetters and the heavy ivory, starved so that the spark of life barely was kept aglow within them, ravaged by weakness and disease and the strain of marching, and overborne by the hopelessness and misery of their position, they died by the thousands. For those who lagged beneath the weight of misfortunes there was the whip; and when the lash could urge no longer, and the victim sank to the ground with the tusk he had carried for hundreds of miles fallen beside him, . . . there was the Arab sword, . . . long, straight, double-edged and sharp as any razor . . . .

The most notorious of the Arab slavers in the 19th century was Hamed bin Muhammed. The Africans whom he terrorized called him Tipoo Tib, and this is the name by which he has become known. Tipoo Tib means "the sound of guns," a sound which the natives had learned to associate with the Arab's slave-raiding expeditions to the interior. Throughout most of the last half of the 19th century he dominated the East African trade in slaves and ivory. He was so crafty that at one time in his career he managed to have himself appointed sultan of a tribe in the Congo and thus gained control of a territory so vast that his subjects probably numbered over a million.

Ruthless in all his dealings with the Africans, Tipoo Tib was always courteous and helpful to Europeans whose

An Arab slave coffle. The forked logs to which the captives are tied served to keep the coffle together. At the height of their power, Arab traders exported about 30,000 slaves yearly from East Africa. It has been estimated that more than 100,000 of their captives never lived to reach the sea.

power he respected. For instance, he gave valuable assistance to the explorers Livingston, Stanley, and Cameron during their journeys through Africa. Indeed, if we want to set the historical records straight, we should note that this slaver was probably the first non-African to visit most of the areas of East and Central Africa supposedly discovered by the 19th-century European explorers.

Apparently Tipoo Tib never regretted his long career as a slaver. When Europeans complained of his cruelty, he accused them of being self-righteous and referred to the Bible as the authority for his actions. He once pointed out to an English missionary that "Abraham, Isaac, and Jacob made many slaves, and God did not punish them." With his death in 1905, the most daring and ruthless scourge of Africans passed from the scene.

Tipoo Tib and the other Arab traders used black slaves primarily for carting ivory, but they also forced them to serve in other ways. Some of the male slaves were trained as soldiers and used in raiding expeditions against their own people. The African soldiers often became Muslims and were accepted as part of Arab society. African women were either sold to be concubines in the Arab harems, or to be domestic servants. Some of the boys were castrated to become eunuchs for the harems.

At the height of the slave raids in East Africa, about 30,000 slaves were exported annually, most of them to buyers in Arabia, Brazil, and Cuba. When the slave trade was curtailed on the west coast in the early 19th century, European and American slavers bought slaves from the Arabs until the final suppression of the trade came with the establishment of colonial governments in the area. Even so, the beautiful island of Zanzibar quietly carried on commerce in slaves under the very nose of the British Resident until 1964, when its Sultan was overthrown in an African-led revolution and many Arabs were massacred.

Apparently slavery and the slave trade still exist in some parts of the modern Arab world. Although Saudi Arabia officially abolished slavery in 1964, evidence indicates that the institution has survived; for instance, there have been reports of black African Muslims being kidnapped and sold as slaves while they were on pilgrimage to Mecca. Such incidents do not improve relations between the African and Arab worlds. When Arab leaders cannot understand the hostility of some Africans toward the Arab nations, it may be worthwhile to remind them that the Arabs' part in enslaving black people is an injury not easily forgotten.

SLAVERY
still exists!

- It exists in 30 countries of the 'free' world
- In one country alone 1,000,000 live as serfs
- In another country one harem contains 300 women
- Children are still being sold into drudgery
- The UN Convention on Slavery is openly flouted

The ANTI-SLAVERY SOCIETY still exists!

Started in 1823, the Society's continued existence is a reminder of a task unfinished. Please help us to end slavery once and for all. For free information write to the Chairman, **Sir Douglas Glover TD,MP Anti-Slavery Society, Denison House, 296 Vauxhall Bridge Road, London, SW1   Telephone: 01-834 6065**

A poster issued in 1970 by the British Anti-Slavery Society.

5

Abolition of the Slave Trade

Slavery was not abolished in ancient Greece or Rome nor in any of the other great ancient and medieval civilizations of the world. But we know that the system weakened the Roman Empire and contributed to its eventual overthrow by the barbarians. Any society in which a large slave population supports an upper class of free men carries in it the seeds of its own destruction. Still, the lessons of history are not easy to learn. It seems that nature has limited the range of human intelligence but has set no bounds to human stupidity. So slavery continued to exist throughout the modern world, supported by men and women who should have known better, until some dedicated people decided to end it.

In 1700 Samuel Sewall, justice of the Massachusetts Supreme Court, wrote a pamphlet called The Selling of Joseph, *one of the earliest anti-slavery appeals to be published in North America. In it he argued that Africans, despite their black skins, were "sons and daughters of the first Adam" and thus entitled to liberty.*

Early Opposition to Slavery in North America

Some of the earliest attempts to restrict or abolish slavery and the traffic in slaves took place in the British colonies in North America during the 17th century. In 1641, Massachusetts passed a law forbidding the admission into the colony of all slaves except captives in war and those who sold themselves for debts. Rhode Island in 1652 made it illegal for anyone to be enslaved for life; a slave was to be freed after 10 years or, if he had been born a slave, after the age of 24.

Such colonial restrictions on slavery were most often prompted by fear of slave uprisings. There were some religious sects in the colonies, however, which were opposed to slavery on principle. Foremost among them were the

Quakers. As early as the founding of Pennsylvania in 1681 by a Quaker, William Penn (himself a slave owner), most Quakers had refused to enslave any human being. (The Quakers were a persecuted sect in England and their own children were often sold into slavery as a form of religious persecution.) In 1688 a group of Quakers in Pennsylvania issued a proclamation condemning slavery in every form. By 1712 they had persuaded the colonial assembly to enact laws restricting the importation of slaves into the colony. However, the measures were vetoed by the government in England. Vested interests in the slave trade at home were too strong.

One of the outstanding fighters for abolition was the French-born Quaker, Anthony Benezet, who lived in Pennsylvania. In 1772 he persuaded a meeting of Pennsylvania Quakers to condemn the slave trade by vote. Benezet was a man of great influence. He became the friend of Benjamin Franklin and Benjamin Rush, both opponents of slavery, and corresponded with many of the British abolitionists. His book *Some Historical Accounts of Guinea* inspired the sermons of John Wesley against slavery. Another book, *Short Account of That Part of Africa Inhabited by Negroes*, influenced Thomas Clarkson to become an ardent abolitionist. Benezet's works were also very influential in France and contributed to the abolitionist movement there.

Although some of the colonists in America felt the need for abolishing or restricting the slave trade in the 18th century and even passed laws against it, they were overruled by George III, who forbade the British government to assent to any such laws. It might have been expected, however, that when the colonies declared their independence, slavery would finally have been abolished by law. But this

Jefferson's first draft of the Declaration of Independence contained an attack against slavery and the slave trade which proved unacceptable to the Southern colonies.

proved impossible since many of the rebellious colonists were still slave owners.

Some of the leading figures of the Revolutionary period were sincerely opposed to slavery. Jefferson's first draft of the Declaration of Independence had contained a clause which claimed that George III had "waged cruel war against human nature itself, violating its most sacred rights of life and liberty in the persons of a distant people who never offended him, captivating and carrying them into slavery in another hemisphere. . . ." Jefferson's accusation against the

English king was somewhat unrealistic, since it completely disregarded the active American participation in the slave trade. However, its implications were plain. The clause was omitted from the Declaration at the insistence of Georgia and South Carolina.

At the end of the Revolution, the new American government warned the British against exporting slaves into the United States. Many states also took legal action to limit or abolish slavery. Virginia in 1778 and Maryland in 1783 enacted laws against bringing slaves into their states to sell. Pennsylvania passed a law for the gradual abolition of slavery in 1780. By 1783, slavery had been abolished in Massachusetts by judicial decision; the Massachusetts courts decreed that the institution was obviously illegal, since the state constitution had declared that "all men are born free and equal." In 1786, New Jersey passed a manumission act and North Carolina imposed a heavy duty on slave imports. In 1787 South Carolina banned the importation of slaves for five years. During this same year, the Continental Congress, acting under the Articles of Confederation, forbade the existence of slavery in the territory northwest of the Ohio River.

Despite the concern expressed by Congress and the various states, slavery and the slave trade did not become major issues at the Constitutional Convention assembled in Philadelphia in 1787. Some influential people at the time believed that slavery as an institution was uneconomical and would soon disappear from the American scene. (In 1787, cotton had not yet come to dominate the economy of the South.) Nevertheless, Southern delegates to the Convention were opposed to any consideration of slavery that might bring up the question of abolition. Although several clauses in the finished Constitution dealt with slavery, the word "slave" was carefully avoided. Article I, Section 2 contained the famous "three-fifths compromise," an agreement to count five slaves as the equivalent of three free persons for purposes of taxation and the apportionment of representatives in Congress. A fugitive slave provision was written into Article IV, Section 2, and at the insistence of Georgia and South Carolina, a clause forbidding the federal government to abolish the slave trade before the year 1808 was also adopted by the convention (Article I, Section 9).

George Washington addressing the Constitutional Convention in Philadelphia, 1787. The Constitution guaranteed "the blessings of liberty" to all the people of the United States except slaves, who were excluded from its protection.

Toussaint L'Ouverture, a self-educated black slave, was one of the leaders of the Haitian rebellion. He became ruler of the island in 1799 but was defeated and imprisoned by the French several years later.

In its final form, the constitution of the nation founded on a belief that all men are created equal did little to promote the abolition of slavery or the slave trade. However, there were other historical forces at work during the last decade of the 18th century which contributed to that end. In 1791 a slave revolt broke out in the French colony of Saint-Domingue, or Haiti, on the West Indian island of Hispaniola. The uprising was long and bloody and eventually brought the whole island under the domination of the black majority. It led Napoleon to sell the Louisiana territory to the United States and struck fear into most of the Southern states which had large slave populations. So a number of laws restricting the importation of slaves were passed in Georgia and South Carolina, and care was taken to prevent slave uprisings. But it was fear, and not humanity, which led to the passage of these measures.

The Abolitionist Movement in Great Britain

In Great Britain, the abolitionist movement made progress during the second half of the 18th century. Among the early abolitionists was Grenville Sharp, whose efforts on behalf of fugitive slaves in England led to an important court decision. In 1765, the master of one of the slaves whom Sharp had aided brought a lawsuit against the abolitionist for stealing his property. The suit was eventually dropped, but Sharp persisted in his efforts to get a court judgment on a similar case involving a fugitive slave. He succeeded finally in 1772, when Lord Chief Justice Mansfield handed down the decision in the Somersett case that "as soon as any slave sets foot on English ground he becomes free."

Though Mansfield's judgment struck a blow at the legality of slavery, it did not, as most people tend to believe, abolish the institution of slavery in England. That could only be done by the legislature. It was possible for such a judgment to approach the validity of law within England, where there was no slave population. But it could not prevent slave ships from sailing from British ports or from entering them, and it did not abolish slavery in the British Empire.

The real drive for abolition of the slave trade was provided by Thomas Clarkson and William Wilberforce. Clarkson was the son of a clergyman and had a small private income. He had hoped to become a minister but had been attracted to the cause of abolition after reading Benezet's *Short Account*. In 1785, while attending Cambridge University, Clarkson won a Latin Prize for an essay entitled "Is it lawful to make others slaves against their will?"

Soon after, he had a vision which urged him on to his eventual goal of abolition. He settled in London, revived the dormant Quaker Committee for the Abolition of Slavery, and reorganized it. In 1787, with Grenville Sharp, Josiah Wedgwood, and others, Clarkson founded the Society for the Abolition of the Slave Trade. The Society's seal pictured an African in chains, "kneeling with one knee upon the ground, and with both hands lifted up to Heaven." Around the seal was the inscription "Am I not a Man and a Brother?" This seal was copied in china by Wedgwood, who was a potter, and sold in the thousands.

This medallion or cameo, created by the famous potter Josiah Wedgwood, provided valuable publicity for the British abolitionists. Mounted on hatpins, stickpins, and rings, the cameo became a popular adornment for fashionable people who supported the antislavery cause.

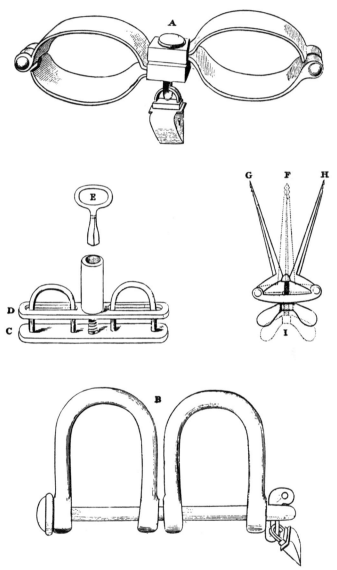

Tools of the slave trade: (A) handcuffs used to shackle one slave to another; (B) leg shackles; (C-E) the thumbscrew, an instrument of persuasion; (F-I) the "speculum oris," or mouth opener, used on slaves who refused to eat. (Illustration from Clarkson's book Abolition of the Slave Trade*)*

In undertaking with the zeal of a fanatic to abolish the slave trade, Clarkson was exposing his life to grave dangers. He visited the slave ports of Liverpool and Bristol, where he talked to people connected with the traffic and collected some of the instruments of the trade—shackles, handcuffs, thumbscrews, and mouth openers. Once while in Liverpool he was attacked for interfering in other men's business, but he managed to escape and returned to continue his investigations.

What Clarkson needed for his crusade was a dedicated fellow-worker with independent means who was also an orator. Such an assistant he found in William Wilberforce, the son of a rich Yorkshire merchant. Wilberforce was a brilliant, sickly man who had inherited a fortune which he devoted to fighting the trade. He had very influential friends, among whom were William Pitt, who became Prime Minister at the age of 22, Charles Fox, the able English politician, and Benjamin Franklin. Wilberforce himself entered Parliament at the age of 21 but soon became bored with political life. However, Pitt persuaded him to keep his seat in the legislature and he began to take an interest in the cause of abolition. Eventually, the Society for the Abolition of the Slave Trade asked him to be their spokesman in Parliament. From then on a close friendship developed between Wilberforce and Clarkson.

The British abolitionists had to be realistic in their methods. It was obvious that powerful economic and financial groups would be affected by the abolition of the slave trade and would put up a determined fight to protect their interests. So Clarkson decided to stress the point that the traffic in slaves brought untold hardships to British seamen, whose sufferings at the time were proverbial. He did not

Thomas Clarkson addressing a convention of the World Anti-Slavery Society in London, 1840.

forget the sufferings of the Africans but felt that if he laid stress on that aspect of the trade he would win little or no sympathy from his countrymen. He also tried to assure the West Indian planters that domestic slavery would continue.

To support his case against the cruelty of the slave trade, Clarkson collected much detailed information on the treatment of sailors and their condition on board the slave ships. The evidence was not easy to obtain, since the trading interests often interfered with potential witnesses. But Clarkson was a determined man and could not be easily discouraged. His work did not stop.

The British abolitionists, led by Wilberforce and Clarkson, carried on their campaign with such vigor that, on the strength of the numerous petitions sent to Parliament, a Committee of the Privy Council was appointed in 1788 to hear complaints against the trade. Meanwhile, Parliament passed a law limiting the number of slaves that a ship could carry. Then in 1789 Wilberforce presented a series of resolutions calling for the abolition of the trade. This move led to the Parliamentary hearings of 1790 and 1791, during which every aspect of the slave trade was examined.

In France the *Societé des Amis du Noir*—Society of the Friends of Black Men—had been formed by a group of philosophers and aristocrats with liberal views. Clarkson made contact with them and visited Paris in 1789 to solicit support, but he did not meet with much success. He was regarded by some Frenchmen as an English spy who wanted to ruin French sugar interests in the West Indies. Others felt that he was giving encouragement to rebellious slaves in some of the French colonies. Though influential leaders like Mirabeau and Lafayette supported Clarkson, and Mirabeau introduced a bill to abolish the slave trade, the French national assembly refused to pass it until the British Parliament had first passed a similar bill.

The French Revolution began in 1789 and the resulting agitation was felt throughout Europe. The antislavery cause in England was injured by its association with the disruptive forces of revolution. Clarkson and the other abolitionists lost support because of the events in France and the slave insurrections which they sparked off in Martinique and Saint-Domingue. Yet Wilberforce continued his efforts in Parliament by introducing a bill in 1791 to prohibit the importation of slaves into the British West Indies. The bill was defeated. Although Wilberforce had to contend with hostility against his cause aroused by the events of the time, he did not give up the fight.

During this period the abolitionists' attempts to end the slave trade were continually frustrated by their opponents' determined efforts to preserve it. The methods adopted by the proslavery forces were familiar. Money was collected by the West Indian planters and their supporters to fight abolition bills in Parliament. Witnesses were brought from Africa and the West Indies to maintain that the institution of slavery was benevolent. At one time a letter from the king of Dahomey describing African treatment of captives

The city of Liverpool in the early 19th century. This busy port on the Mersey River dominated the British slave trade during the 50 years preceding its abolition. The frugal merchants of Liverpool refined the techniques of slaving and grew rich on the profits.

was read in Parliament. The document was supposed to show that since human life was valueless in Africa, slavery in the West Indies should be considered a blessing for the Africans. But in spite of this opposition the abolitionists stood their ground. They won added support from the nonconformist religious sects, one of whose leaders, the Methodist John Wesley, had been preaching against the trade.

The first decade of the 19th century was a time of conflict and crisis in Great Britain. During most of these years the nation was at war with the conqueror Napoleon, who had gained control of France, and most of Europe, after the French Revolution. However, the cause of abolition in England was not abandoned even in this turbulent period. In 1806 Charles Fox, the British foreign secretary, introduced a resolution "that effectual measures should be taken for the abolition of the African slave trade." The resolution was passed by a large majority in the House of Commons. Then, after Fox's death that same year, William Grenville introduced a bill in the House of Lords which provided for the abolition of "all manner of dealing and trading in the Purchase, Sale, Barter or Transfer of Slaves." Both Houses of Parliament passed it, and Wilberforce was given a standing ovation. The law became effective in 1807; after May 1 of that year no slave ship could leave an English port. After March 1, 1808, no slave could be landed in a British possession.

At first the penalty for slaving by British subjects was confiscation, but in 1811 a law was passed making the offense a felony whose penalty was transportation to a penal colony. This had the desired effect of stopping British ships from engaging in the trade.

Abolition of the Slave Trade in the United States

In the United States the revolt of the slaves in Haiti led to a number of antislavery laws passed by various states at the end of the 18th century. The fear of a possible epidemic of slave revolts was so great that the importation of West Indian Negroes was prohibited in most states. Despite the stiff penalties imposed by these laws, however, the illicit traffic in slaves continued.

With the example of the states to spur them on, Congress attempted to deal with the question of the slave trade at the federal level. During the first session in 1789 a bill designed to make the importation of slaves unprofitable was introduced. It met with opposition and was withdrawn. The same bill was reintroduced in 1790 as a result of petitions from abolitionists, among them the Quakers, who urged Congress to inquire "whether, notwithstanding such seeming impediments, it be not in reality within your power to exercise justice and mercy, which, if adhered to, . . . must produce the abolition of the slave trade." The measure was opposed on the grounds that it would interfere with the rights of property holders in the Southern states. However, it had the backing of James Madison, who wanted to see "if anything is within the federal authority to restrain such violation of the rights of nations and mankind, as is supposed to be practiced in some parts of the United States." The motion was also supported by a petition from the Pennsylvania Society for Promoting the Abolition of Slavery, signed by its president, Benjamin Franklin. The petition asked Congress to "step up to the very verge of the power vested in you for discouraging every species of traffic in the persons of our fellow-men." This evidence of support led to the second reading of the resolution. Southerners considered the measure unconstitutional and spoke out

In 1788 Benjamin Franklin, then 82 years old, was elected president of the first antislavery society in the United States. Franklin's last public act before his death in April 1790 was the signing of a petition to Congress calling for an end to the slave trade.

against it, but their arguments were met with more forcible ones from the opponents of slavery.

When the different views had been expressed, Congress voted on the motion and approved it by 43 votes to 11; among those opposed were the representatives of South Carolina, Georgia, Virginia, Maryland, and New York. A committee was formed to draw up a proposal for the House, and the result was a watered-down Declaration of Powers of Congress. It provided that slaves could be imported into the states in which slavery was legal until 1808, when Congress could prohibit the traffic. The federal government could not interfere in the freeing or the treatment of slaves within the states. (This was a right presumably reserved to the states by the Constitution.) Congress could prevent citizens of the United States from engaging in the slave trade in Africa on behalf of foreign powers and could enforce humane treatment of slaves during their passage to the United States. It could also prevent foreigners from fitting out ships in any United States port for transporting African slaves to any foreign port.

The question of states rights, which was later to plague American politics and to give legal sanction to the ill-treatment of Negroes, became crucial during this period. Although further petitions protesting the trade came to Congress after the Declaration of Powers, they were resisted until the threat of a slave uprising led to the Act of 1794. This act was designed only "to prohibit the carrying on the Slave Trade from the United States to any foreign place or country."

Then in 1800 Representative Waln of Pennsylvania presented a petition from some free Negroes in his state, asking for a revision of the slave trade and fugitive slave laws, and for eventual emancipation. During the debates that followed the introduction of the petition, the familiar economic arguments were presented, as well as the usual contention that Negroes gained rather than suffered by being enslaved. Eventually, a law was enacted which prohibited citizens of the United States from having any interest, direct or indirect, in slaving voyages or serving on slave ships in any capacity. After the successful Haitian revolt of 1803 an act was passed providing for the seizure of ships bringing "any negro, mulatto, or other person of colour" into states which had prohibited the slave trade.

Despite such measures, the slave trade continued to flourish throughout this period. In 1803 South Carolina repealed its ban on importing slaves, thus ushering in a new period of slaving activity. The newly acquired territory of Louisiana also joined in the traffic, which increased enormously. It was not until 1807 that Congress finally passed an act prohibiting the slave trade on the national level. The act became law on January 1, 1808. It was a landmark in the struggle for emancipation, but it took a civil war to abolish the legal status of slavery itself in the United States. Those who gained from the trade were determined to break the law against it, and since slavery was accepted in various states, the lawbreakers had greater public support than their counterparts in Great Britain.

In Europe, Denmark abolished the slave trade in 1802, Sweden in 1813, the Netherlands in 1814, and France in 1818.

6

The Illegal Slave Trade

Since the various European and American nations passed laws abolishing the slave trade at different times, it was to be expected that the traffic in slaves would continue for many years. The Portuguese, the Spaniards, and the Arabs had not agreed to abolish the trade, so they could supply any nation that wanted slaves with as many as were required. Moreover, the illegal trading in slaves was bound to continue since the institution of slavery itself had not been declared illegal in the West Indies, South America, the United States, Africa, and Arabia.

In the United States the need for slaves was greatly increased by the invention of the cotton gin in 1793. The dangers involved in breaking the law were compensated for by the huge profits which could be made. As a result, the traffic in slaves to the United States doubled in volume in the period from 1807 to 1840. During these years many shiploads of slaves were smuggled into the Southern states; pirates like Jean Lafitte also joined in the trade by capturing slave ships and selling their cargoes to American buyers.

The increased activity in slave trading during this period was also influenced by the developing economies of other American countries. The rapid expansion of the sugar plantations in Cuba made an increase in the labor force necessary, and the Spaniards imported more slaves to meet the demand. Brazil also needed slaves for her coffee plantations and copper mines. Even though she signed a treaty prohibiting the trade in 1829, its provisions were ignored; thousands of slaves were brought into Brazil during the very year in which the treaty was supposed to take effect.

It was soon realized that legal measures alone could not stop people from engaging in the slave trade. The African chiefs and kings whose greed had been aroused by the European and American traders continued to fight to get slaves. They thought it an invasion of their rights to be asked by any nation to stop enslaving their kith and kin. The fact that the trade was illegal had led to an increase in the selling price of slaves and to higher profits for the slave traders. The price of slaves on the cotton plantations was very high, but the purchase price in Africa was low because the embargo kept many potential buyers away from the Guinea Coast.

The contraband traffic in slaves flourished because Great Britain was the only nation which took the suppression of the international trade seriously. The powerful British navy patrolled the seas from the Atlantic to the Indian Ocean, but it could not cope with all the ships which took part in the illegal trade. Most of the British patrol ships were slow-moving vessels used in the Napoleonic wars. The slave merchants used small, fast ships called clippers, built in the United States, which could usually outrun the larger British craft.

In 1817, Great Britain signed a treaty with Spain which provided that each nation could search the other's ships for contraband in waters north of the equator. The British government made a similar agreement with Portugal in the same year. However, since the British right of search did not apply to vessels navigating south of the equator, nations which had abolished the trade could still transport slaves illegally in southern waters under the Portuguese and Spanish flags. The Netherlands, Sweden, and France signed similar treaties with Britain in 1818, 1824, and 1831 respectively, but the United States refused to enter into such an agreement. British interference with American shipping had been the major cause of a minor war between the two nations which took place in the years 1812 to 1814. Accordingly, the United States was very reluctant to give any nation, and particularly Great Britain, the right to stop and search vessels flying the American flag. Because of this reluctance it was possible for American ships to be used in the contraband slave trade during the years following the War of 1812.

It was not until 1820 that the British persuaded the United States to station her own warships in West Africa to check American vessels suspected of carrying slaves. But the American navy was also faced with the problem of slavers using flags of different nationalities, so the ships were withdrawn after three years. Great Britain then tried to sign a treaty with the United States declaring slave trading as piracy, and thus subject to international law, but the measure was defeated by Congress. So the traffic continued with the tacit blessing of the United States government. In fact, American consuls in foreign ports often issued the necessary papers to European traders who wanted the protection of the American government while transporting slaves. Ship captains desiring this security would simply buy a vessel registered in the United States. The American consul would then provide a bill of sale for the ship, instead of having the register transferred, so the vessel could continue to sail under the American flag.

The British patrol ship H.M.S. Primrose captures a Portuguese slaver. Great Britain's determined efforts to end the slave trade and the equal determination of other nations to continue it created confusion and conflict on the high seas.

It is estimated that during this period the international trade increased from 100,000 slaves annually to 200,000. It was obvious that, as Governor Buchanan of Liberia reported in 1839, "the chief obstacle to the success of the very active measures pursued by the British government for the suppression of the slave trade on the coast is the American flag." These abuses could have been stopped if the United States had agreed to a mutual right of search with Great Britain. But this right was disputed to such an extent that it seemed the two nations might go to war again to settle their differences.

Eventually, the serious international disputes arising from several slave mutinies in the early 1840s led the United States to agree to a treaty for the "final suppression" of the slave trade. The Webster-Ashburton Treaty of 1842 provided for joint cruising of American and British warships on the African coast; ships flying the American flag would be pursued by the American navy, and those flying any other flag by the British navy. However, the United States, largely because of the state of slavery at home, did not take the treaty seriously. Though both nations undertook to station adequate naval squadrons in the areas concerned, the United States reduced the size of her squadron gradually until by 1857 it consisted of no more than seven ships. Moreover, the American ships were stationed at Cape Verde, far away from the scene of vigorous activity.

The main reason for the inactivity of the American fleet was the fact that the squadrons were sent out not to suppress the trade but to prevent the British from attempting to board ships flying the American flag. The fear that Great Britain was trying to impose her will on the United States was greater than the nation's desire to end slavery.

Perhaps if the British squadrons had been permitted by the African rulers to land on their territories and free the slaves kept in the coastal storehouses, the work of the blockading teams would have shown better results. But the kings had a vested interest in the trade, and the question of abolition had not arisen in Africa. In the decade of the 1840s, the British Foreign Office tried to restrict the traffic in slaves by signing treaties with various African kings, but the agreements were generally ignored. For example, the king of Bonny agreed to abandon the trade in return for an annual subsidy of $10,000 and then continued to capture and sell slaves. King Gezo of Dahomey complained that Queen Victoria could help him more by sending guns with which to capture slaves than by urging him to end the trade. It is an uncomfortable and ironic fact that the African traffic in slaves did not end until colonialism was firmly established by the very European nations which had brought the trade to the continent originally. Perhaps colonialism did have one good result.

The Spaniards and the Portuguese ignored all the treaties they signed with the British, and the trade in Cuba and Brazil reached its peak in the 1840s. Then in 1849 Great Britain sent a 'squadron under the command of Admiral Reynolds to stop the Brazilian slave trade. Reynolds was instructed to seize and burn all the slave ships he could find. He carried out his duties so faithfully that in 1851 Lord Palmerston, the British foreign secretary, could tell Parliament that the Brazilian trade had ended. It was revived on a smaller scale after the British left in 1853, and there were reports of slave ships sighted in Brazilian waters as late as the 1880s. The Cuban trade continued unchecked after 1850, often under the protection of the American flag.

The Arab-controlled slave traffic on the east coast of Africa lasted considerably longer than the west coast trade. The slaves shown in this photograph were rescued from an Arab slaver off Zanzibar in the year 1884.

The slave traffic on the east coast of Africa continued without a break until the end of the century. The Arab traders supplied slaves and ivory to the United States, Brazil, and Arabia for as long as the demand lasted and the profit remained high. Not until the European powers established colonies in the area was the East African slave trade checked. However, as we have noted earlier, European suppression of Arab slaving was never completely effective.

7

Abolition of the Institution of Slavery

The illegal trade in slaves continued during the first half of the 19th century because the institution of slavery had not been abolished by the majority of slaving nations. The British could afford to make slavery illegal in Great Britain, but they found it more difficult to abolish the institution in their West Indian colonies. There slavery had become the basis of economic and political life. Once the British government and Parliament decided to end the system, however, no amount of opposition could stop them.

In 1823 a society for the Mitigation and Gradual Abolition of Slavery Throughout the British Dominions was founded in England under the leadership of a member of Parliament, Thomas F. Buxton. Other societies aimed at bettering the condition of slaves also sprang up, but it was not until 1825 that the crusade against slavery got under way. Some free Negroes joined in this crusade because they felt that their freedom was worth nothing so long as slavery existed as an institution. In the colonies of Jamaica and Antigua, the free blacks opposed all schemes for the betterment of the conditions of slaves and instead pressed for complete emancipation.

The opposition forces were still very strong, but in 1833 the British government decided to abolish slavery by paying compensation to slave owners. However, the slave's emancipation was not complete; the law provided for a system of apprenticeship which would serve as a transition from slavery to freedom. The freedmen were to remain under the supervision of special magistrates appointed by the British government and were to enjoy certain privileges, but not the full rights of citizenship. Indignities like flogging persisted, and the freedmen continued to be exploited. The West Indian planters were opposed to complete emancipation, but the abolitionists eventually won. In 1838 the apprenticeship system was ended in the British colonies and Negroes became free and responsible citizens.

Conflict over Abolition in the United States

The British could afford to disrupt an economic system which had lasted over three centuries because they had an alternative to slave labor in indentured laborers from India and China. These people were transported to the British colonies to work on the estates which had employed slaves before. (The seeds of the modern racial problem in Guyana, the former colony of British Guiana, were sown at that time.) In the United States, however, the situation was

Slaves operating a cotton gin. This machine, invented by Eli Whitney, separated the cotton fibers from the seeds by means of toothed cylinders turned by a crank. With the aid of the gin, a slave could process 50 pounds of cotton in the same time that it would have taken him to clean a single pound by hand.

different. The invention of the cotton gin in 1793 had caused a boom in the cotton trade, and the need for slaves was greater than ever. Moreover, there appeared to be no readily available alternative to slave labor in the American South. To talk of abolishing the system under such conditions seemed like madness to Southern planters and politicians. The period between 1808 and the Civil War was one in which the South tried to revive the slave trade and to make the institution of slavery permanent, while the North tried to eliminate both.

A primary objective of the South's strategy was the repeal of the 1808 law which had abolished the African slave trade. In the late 1850s the Southern states held commercial conventions to decide on the course of action to be taken in achieving this goal. The convention of 1858 resolved that "slavery is right, and that being right, there can be no wrong in the natural means to its formation," and therefore that "it is expedient and proper that the foreign slave trade should be reopened." During this period the debate also continued in the United States Congress; in December 1856, Southern congressmen tried unsuccessfully to reopen the question of the revival of the African slave trade.

Actually, the apathy of the federal government made it very easy for the Southern states to break most of the existing laws forbidding the importation of slaves. The domestic slave trade also helped to meet the cotton planters' need for slaves. By means of this interstate traffic, slaves were transported from Virginia, Maryland, and the Carolinas, where the supply of laborers greatly exceeded the demand, to the states of the lower South, where the cotton economy was booming. Some slaveholders in the economically depressed areas of the upper South resorted to deliberate slave breeding in order to increase their supply of marketable human stock.

Supplied from these various sources, the number of slaves increased enormously during the early years of the 19th century. It is estimated that in 1790 there were less than 700,000 slaves in the United States. By 1830 the slave

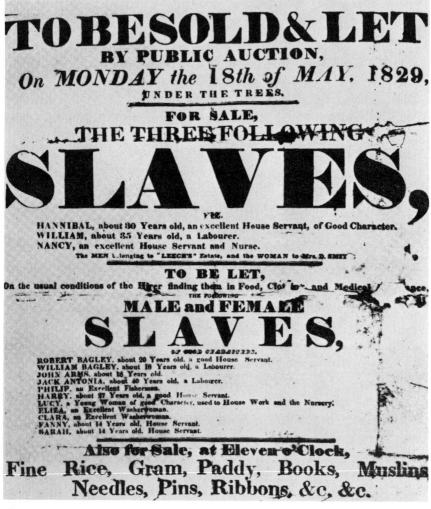

TO BE SOLD & LET

BY PUBLIC AUCTION,

On MONDAY the 18th of MAY, 1829,

UNDER THE TREES.

FOR SALE,

THE THREE FOLLOWING

SLAVES,

VIZ.

HANNIBAL, about 30 Years old, an excellent House Servant, of Good Character.
WILLIAM, about 35 Years old, a Labourer.
NANCY, an excellent House Servant and Nurse.

The MEN belonging to "LEECH'S" Estate, and the WOMAN to Mrs. D. SMIT.

TO BE LET,

On the usual conditions of the Hirer finding them in Food, Clothing and Medical Assistance,

THE FOLLOWING

MALE and FEMALE

SLAVES,

OF GOOD CHARACTERS,

ROBERT BAGLEY, about 20 Years old, a good House Servant.
WILLIAM BAGLEY, about 18 Years old, a Labourer.
JOHN ARMS, about 18 Years old.
JACK ANTONIA, about 40 Years old, a Labourer.
PHILIP, an Excellent Fisherman.
HARRY, about 27 Years old, a good House Servant.
LUCY, a Young Woman of good Character, used to House Work and the Nursery.
ELIZA, an Excellent Washerwoman.
CLARA, an Excellent Washerwoman.
FANNY, about 14 Years old, House Servant.
SARAH, about 14 Years old, House Servant.

Also for Sale, at Eleven o'Clock,

Fine Rice, Gram, Paddy, Books, Muslins Needles, Pins, Ribbons, &c, &c.

Poster announcing a public auction of slaves and other assorted goods. As the sign indicates, slaves were not only sold but also let, or rented. If a master had more workers than he had work, he could hire out some of his slaves for varying periods of time. In this way he could profit from their labor and, at the same time, avoid the expense of maintaining idle slaves.

population was over 2 million. In the 1860 census the number of slaves recorded was 3,953,760; almost half of these lived in the cotton belt of the South—Georgia, Alabama, Tennessee, Mississippi, Arkansas, Louisiana, and Texas.

These numbers indicate that slavery had become an important part of the political, economic, and social life of the South. A description of the institution may provide a clearer picture of Southern reasons for opposing abolition.

There were about 8 million whites in the South in 1860, but only 384,884 were slave owners. However, economic and political power was concentrated in the hands of this minority of citizens who fought to preserve the institution of slavery. Since the economy of the South depended on the plantation system, the owners of slaves had the means to control the political machine. Those Southerners who did not own slaves hoped to obtain some in the future, so the majority accepted the existing economic system.

Slavery in the American South

More than 200,000 slave owners in 1860 had five or fewer slaves; 338,000 owners, or 88 percent of the slave-holding population, had fewer than 20 slaves. These figures show that the ordinary slaveholders, the small planters and farmers, actually owned the majority of slaves in the South. However, the owners of large plantations with 60 or more slaves exerted influence out of proportion to their numbers. The increased productivity of the large cotton plantations contributed to the economic and political power which their owners possessed. In 1860 the Southern states produced a crop of 5,387,000 bales of cotton—seven-eighths of the world's cotton supply. More than 60 percent of the crop was grown in Mississippi, Alabama, Louisiana, and Georgia; these were the states with many plantations having more

Slaves picking cotton in the fields of a Mississippi plantation. The field hands did the hardest work on a plantation and were most apt to feel the blows of the overseer's lash.

than 20 slaves.

To protect their economic assets the Southern states had severe laws known as slave codes. These codes were based on the assumption that slaves were not human beings but property; therefore the laws were designed to protect the property owners and not the slaves. A slave had no legal standing in any court in the United States. He could not

sue or be sued, and he could give evidence only in a case involving a slave or a free Negro. He could not be a party to a contract and had no legal right to own property. A slave could not strike a white person even in self-defense. If a white man killed a slave, he was normally accused of manslaughter, a relatively minor offense. But the rape of a female slave was a serious crime, since the criminal had trespassed on another white man's property.

The slave's personal freedom was drastically limited

$200 REWARD!

Ran away from his owner [a Lady residing near Upper Marlboro, Prince George's County, Md.] on or about the 12th inst. of this month. a bright Mulatto man named Frank, a carpenter by trade, he is about five feet 9 or 10 inches high, light grey eyes, slow in speech. and very good personal appearance, about twenty-five years of age, his clothing good.

One Hundred dollars will be paid if apprehended within thirty miles of home, if more than thirty, the above reward, provided he be secured in Jail so that his owner' gets him again.

W. D. BOWIE,

for the owner,

Buena Vista Post Office, Prince George's Co. Md. February 14th, 1853.

Runaway slaves were a continual problem in the South. In an attempt to explain why slaves persisted in running away from their masters, some Southerners claimed that Africans were prone to a strange disease which made it impossible for them to remain in one place for any length of time.

by the system under which he lived. Slaves could leave a plantation only after obtaining the owner's permission. Any slave who could not show evidence of such permission was liable to be turned over to state officials. In all Southern states slaves were forbidden to carry firearms, and in Mississippi they could not beat drums or blow horns. They were not allowed to hire themselves out or to sell or buy goods. They were forbidden to visit the homes of whites and free Negroes or to entertain them in their own quarters. They could hold assemblies only in the presence of white persons and were not permitted to receive or transmit to others literature calculated to subvert the system of slavery.

Many of the Southern states had special courts which enforced the slave codes; slaves accused of crimes were tried before juries of slaveholders or by justices of the peace. Most offenses were punished by flogging, but capital crimes—arson, raping a white woman, conspiracy to rebel—had penalties of branding, imprisonment, or death. Juries of slaveholders tried to avoid sentencing slaves to death or to long terms in prison, since such penalties deprived fellow slave owners of their property. In general, black people in the South did not receive justice from the courts and were often punished for crimes they did not commit.

Since no slave willingly submits to his condition, slave owners were always faced with the danger of possible conspiracy and rebellion. To check insurrections, patrols made up of whites serving from one to three months guarded various districts in the Southern states. The patrols searched Negro homes for arms, visited slave assemblies to see that no plots were being hatched, and, during emergencies, killed any suspects that they could lay hands on. This patrol system encouraged the lynchings which became a way of life in the South after the slaves' emancipation.

In spite of the elaborate legal codes, slave masters in the South held the real power and dealt with their slaves as they thought fit. The brutal treatment of slaves on many plantations was notorious. Plantation slaves were forced to work under the lash and were at the mercy of often cruel overseers. Sometimes slaves were employed as drivers of other slaves, and these favored individuals carried out the brutal treatment for the white master. The enormous power that the whites had over the slaves was an important cause of the racism which later became a disease in American society.

Many plantation slaves were badly clothed and poorly housed. Their lives were dull and drab, and they had very little free time. On the large estates young slaves under six years of age were allowed to spend their time playing, often with the master's children, but after their sixth birthday they were put to work. The slaves' family life was frequently disrupted because masters could sell individual members of a family at any time.

Most plantation slaves lived in crudely built log cabins with dirt floors. They slept on piles of corn husks, and their food consisted largely of corn meal, salt pork, and molasses.

Religious instruction could be given to slaves only with the permission of their owners. In some places Negro churches were allowed, but in others the slaves were forced to attend white churches to ensure that no inflammatory speeches were made to them. Education of slaves was forbidden by law in most states but was permitted by some plantation owners. Most Southerners believed that Negroes were incapable of intellectual work, and attempts to disprove this theory were not encouraged. Still, schools for Negroes were founded in some places, and there were cases of black people attending schools for whites.

Marriage among slaves in the United States did not have the sanction of law since slaves could not be parties to a legal contract. Moreover, any union between two slaves was basically impermanent because there was no guarantee that a couple would remain together on the same plantation. The master could always sell one of the pair when he chose, so all unions were subject to the slave owner's economic interest. This state of affairs led to promiscuity and indifference to the rights and interests of black women. Slave women were victims of the lust of white men and often bore the master's children. Evidently the lawmakers could not keep their own laws. It seems ironic that those who were largely responsible for the mixture of the races which they so despised should have regarded Negroes as being sexually depraved.

By 1860 there were 411,000 people of mixed white and black parentage in the United States. White masters had varying attitudes toward their mulatto children. Some sold them without any remorse, while others treated them with consideration, even freeing them and giving them property. White wives, however, usually saw such children as symbols

Evidence that white Southerners disapproved of racial mixing in theory rather than in practice can be seen clearly in the faces of these slaves from Louisiana.

of their husbands' moral degradation and sought to be rid of them.

Though the slaves were expected to be docile, this was seldom the case. They naturally resented their position, and when they did not actively rebel, they often shirked their duties or ran away. Many white masters liked to believe that the slaves' spirituals reflected resignation to their fate and hope for a better life in heaven. However, the majority of slaves hoped for emancipation and a better life here on earth. When it did not come, they sometimes resorted to self-mutilation or suicide. Very often desperate slaves attacked their masters and killed them. The system was dangerous and destructive for both masters and slaves, and the idea that blacks were willing victims of enslavement is purely illusory.

The Final Struggle for Emancipation

We have seen how difficult it was to abolish the slave trade in the United States or to persuade the Southern states to accept the idea of the abolition of slavery. Let us now briefly examine the struggle for emancipation which eventually ended in a bloody civil war.

The fear of slave insurrections and the establishment of black-ruled states in Haiti led some politicians in the United States to consider emancipation as a political necessity. The abolitionists, however, were led by moral fervor to demand freedom for all human beings. Although not all black and colored men in the slave-owning societies of the United States, the West Indies, and Brazil were slaves, in most countries even the free man of color was a second-class citizen or not a citizen at all. For instance, during the period of the abolitionist campaign in the United States some Southern states would not allow free Negroes to remain within their territories. It finally became clear to all right-thinking persons that slavery had made the color of the black man's skin an obstacle to his freedom. Therefore, since men are not responsible for their skin color, the only way to end the injustice was to force the issue of abolition.

After the crusade for abolishing the slave trade ended, the abolitionists in the United States turned their attention to the institution itself. At first most of these opponents of slavery were Northerners, but gradually some Southerners joined at the risk of their lives. There were both white and black abolitionists, and gradualists as well as radicals among both races. All worked toward the same goal. They used books, pamphlets, and newspapers to advance their cause, and held public meetings and religious services at which they preached the equality of man. Eventually they gained enough support to organize the escape of slaves from the Southern states to the North, the West, and Canada.

The leading radical abolitionist was a Northerner, William Lloyd Garrison. In an editorial appearing January 1, 1831, in his newspaper, *The Liberator*, Garrison announced his intention to oppose slavery in these words: "I determined, at every hazard, to lift up the standard of emancipation in the eyes of the nation. . . .I am in earnest—I will not equivocate—I will not excuse—I will not retreat a single inch—AND I WILL BE HEARD." And he was indeed heard. The South was as frightened of Garrison's words as the European aristocrats were of Karl Marx's *Communist Manifesto* in 1848.

When Garrison and his followers found that the American Anti-Slavery Society was advocating gradual abolition, they seized control of the organization in 1840 and the abolitionist forces became divided. Garrison's supporters were very strong, especially in New England. However, even in the North the crusade met with strong opposition, some of it from clergymen, and physical attacks were made on members of the group. The abolitionists did not find it easy to hold meetings, and they often had to leave their states for fear of violence. The federal government offered them little protection. Moreover, the fact that some abolitionists seemed to approve the use of violence to destroy a system based on violence lost them the support of many moderate men. But in the end slavery was destroyed only through the violence of war.

Many black people played active roles in the abolitionist movement during this period. Among them was David Walker, a free Negro who lived in Massachusetts. In 1829,

William Lloyd Garrison (left) and Frederick Douglass, leaders of the abolitionist movement in the United States.

Walker published an appeal addressed to American Negroes in which he angrily denounced slavery and called for the violent overthrow of the system. Frederick Douglass, the most outstanding of the black abolitionists, was a fugitive slave who joined the movement in 1841. Douglass's skill as an orator made him a very useful worker, and he acted as a spokesman for the abolitionist cause on many occasions. In 1847 he started his own paper, the *North Star*. This move led to a break with Garrison, but it did not end Douglass's career as an ardent abolitionist.

One of the most important achievements of the abolitionists was the organization of an escape system for slaves, which came to be known as the Underground Railroad. Though the escape of slaves from the South had been going on since the 18th century with the blessing and aid of the Quakers, it was not until the beginning of the 19th century

113

that a systematic organization for the purpose emerged. The Underground Railroad was risky but full of adventure. Almost all the escapes were at night, and various methods were adopted to prevent detection. The Railroad led north and most of the fugitives followed the North Star all the way to Canada, where slavery was illegal. A Quaker, Levi Coffin, earned the unofficial title of President of the Underground Railroad for his work in this cause. He helped at least 3,000 slaves to escape through his home in Indiana. Harriet Tubman, the most successful Negro "conductor" on the Railroad, personally led more than 300 slaves along the dangerous, secret route to freedom. It is estimated that

Levi Coffin and his wife welcome a group of slaves escaping through the Underground Railroad. Dedicated people like the Coffins turned their homes into way stations along the secret route to the North and freedom.

the South lost 100,000 slaves through the Underground Railroad between 1810 and 1850.

Southerners considered the work of the Underground Railroad as part of a Northern plot to wreck their economy. They became increasingly angry at its success and sought ways to strike back at the abolitionists. Southern states made it impossible for any of their inhabitants to speak out against slavery. Southern politicians and writers spread propaganda on the necessity of slavery for the black man as well as for the white man; their arguments were based, as usual, on the Negro's supposed racial inferiority and intellectual shortcomings. The proslavery factions had the blessing of most of the churches in the South. However, sects like the Methodists, Baptists, and Presbyterians, some of whose members held progressive views on slavery, split in two over the issue.

The question of fugitive slaves was settled temporarily by the Compromise of 1850, which abolished the slave trade in the District of Columbia and provided for stronger fugitive slave laws. These provisions did not satisfy the South. Georgia, Mississippi, Alabama, and South Carolina began to talk of secession, unless there was strict enforcement of the fugitive slave laws by all the states of the Union. But this was not possible, since the militant abolitionists were not prepared to relax their efforts to help slaves escape until emancipation had become the law of the land. When *Uncle Tom's Cabin* was published in 1852, the proslavery elements felt that they could no longer live in peace with the antislavery militants. They had too much to lose.

The slavery controversy reached its final stage in 1854, when the issue of the expansion of slavery to the territories once more divided the nation. This issue had always been

If a novel's greatness can be measured in terms of its popularity and its influence on the course of history, then Uncle Tom's Cabin *was indeed the "Greatest Book of the Age."*

central to Northern and Southern arguments about the future of slavery in the United States. It had been temporarily settled by the Missouri Compromise (1820) and again by the Compromise of 1850, but the passage of the Kansas-Nebraska Act in 1854 reopened the question. The act repealed the Missouri Compromise, which had guaranteed that the northern territories of the Louisiana Purchase would enter the Union as free states, and instead provided that the issue of slavery in Kansas and Nebraska would be decided by the inhabitants of the states. This measure angered the North and opened the way for a bitter controversy over the settlement of Kansas by warring pro-slavery and antislavery forces.

The tense situation was made worse by the Supreme Court decision in the case of *Dred Scott* v. *Sanford*, handed down in 1857. The majority opinion of the Court declared that Negroes could not be considered citizens of any state, and that Congress had no constitutional right to regulate slavery in the territories. The decision was hailed in the South but rejected by many Northerners, especially those aligned with the newly formed Republican party, which was firmly opposed to the expansion of slavery.

In 1859 the antagonisms created by the mood of the nation and the maneuvering of politicians were brought to violent life by the actions of one man. In October of that year, John Brown and a few followers attempted to start a slave insurrection in the South. Brown's efforts were unsuccessful, and he was quickly captured, convicted of treason, and executed. However, the impact of Brown's act on the nation did not end with his death. The South was shocked by the threat of violence so close to home and by the always dreaded possibility of a slave revolt. Southerners were also alarmed by the fact that the antislavery forces in the North apparently approved of John Brown's violent deed and considered him a martyr to their cause. At his trial Brown had accepted the verdict of death with these moving words: "Now, if it is deemed necessary that I should forfeit my life for the furtherance of the ends of justice and mingle my blood . . . with the blood of millions in this slave country whose rights are disregarded by wicked, cruel and unjust enactments, I say, let it be done." Many moderate abolitionists were now convinced that bloodshed such as Brown had promised would inevitably come.

When the election of 1860 brought the Republican party and Abraham Lincoln to power, the Southern states were prepared to act. In December 1860, South Carolina seceded from the Union; within the next six weeks the other states of the deep South also adopted ordinances of secession. The nation was divided and ready for war.

The Civil War began on April 12, 1861, when the forces of the Confederacy fired on Fort Sumter in Charleston harbor. It ended almost four years later, on April 9, 1865, at Appomattox Court House in southern Virginia. During the course of the war, President Lincoln issued the Emancipation Proclamation, which freed all slaves living in states not under the control of the federal government. This decree, which took effect January 1, 1863, was largely a military measure designed to put pressure on the rebellious states, but it did commit Lincoln's administration to a policy of emancipation. The work of abolition was completed after the war with the adoption of the Thirteenth Amendment to the Constitution, in December 1865. After this time the black man in the United States was a person under the law.

Some Americans believed that John Brown was a martyr to a heroic cause; others thought that he was a madman. Observers in both the North and the South interpreted Brown's character and his actions at Harpers Ferry in the light of their own attitudes toward slavery.

119

Abolition of Slavery in Latin America

The elimination of slavery in most of the countries of Latin America was not accompanied by the violence which led to the final abolition of the institution in the United States. In many of the Spanish colonies, the issue of abolition was closely related to the movement for independence. Revolutionary leaders encouraged slave revolts and offered freedom to those slaves who joined them. The resulting internal confusion made it more difficult for Spain to maintain her hold on the rebellious colonies. Negroes fought for freedom in Venezuela, Uruguay, and Cuba, so they could not be denied personal freedom by law when political independence came.

In 1824 the five countries of Central America, which had formed a political confederation after winning their independence, passed an emancipation law freeing the 1,000 slaves in the area. This measure was significant because it was the first of its kind enacted in the Americas. Other Latin American countries took similar action in the following years. Mexico, under President Guerrero, abolished slavery in 1829; Bolivia emancipated her slaves in 1831, Uruguay in 1842. Colombia and Argentina followed suit in 1855, but it was not until 1886 that slaves in Cuba were freed. Brazil was the last Latin American country to abolish slavery. Emancipation in the former Portuguese colony was carried out gradually: in 1831 all slaves of foreign origin living in Brazil were freed; then in 1871 a decree was passed freeing all children born to slave mothers after that year; the remaining 700,000 Brazilian slaves were finally emancipated in 1888.

We need not deceive ourselves that the slave's path to

freedom in Latin America was always smooth. Abolition was opposed vigorously by those who had vested interests in the institution of slavery. However, the fact that freedom for slaves did not result in wars and violent upheavals was due largely to the attitude of white Latin Americans toward black people. Over the centuries, they had regarded Negroes as human beings, had lived closely with them, and had formed unions with them, thus creating a mixed race. Therefore racial "purity" was not a crucial issue in Latin America. The problems caused by freeing the slaves were primarily political and economic, not racial. Although the white man still held the upper hand in most countries, black people had great influence in Brazil, where there was a large Negro and mulatto population. In no part of Latin America did abolition lead to the creation of a "Negro problem" like that which developed in the United States.

8

Legacy of Slavery and the Slave Trade

The long history of slavery in the world does no credit to the intelligence of the human race. The commercial traffic in Africans during the modern era degraded the inhabitants of that continent to the level of beasts. It led to the all-too-common association of the black man's color with that which is sordid and unpleasant in this imperfect world. The inferior social and economic position of black people in many modern societies is due largely to the influence of the slave trade.

The existence of slavery and of the trade that supplied slaves for the world market directly affected the peoples and nations of Africa in many ways, almost all of them harmful. One serious effect of the trade was the depopulation of the continent. No one can say exactly how many people were involved in this great human tragedy, but it has been estimated that over 25 million Africans were successfully transported across the seas to Europe, the Americas, and the West Indies. Another 10 million were taken to Arabia and Asia, while over 10 million lost their lives at sea. The number of fatalities does not include those who died in the interior during the raids, and during the march to the coast. By means of the slave trade, Africa was deprived of many of her most vigorous and productive people and thus weakened and left an easy prey to European powers.

African captives begin the long march to the sea under the watchful eyes of Arab slave traders. Millions of black people were forced to follow this same route to a life of slavery in foreign lands.

The devastation caused by the slave trade clearly paved the way for European colonization in Africa, a development which had disastrous results for Africans in the modern era. Although the northern portions of the continent had been a melting pot of the races and civilizations of Africa, Europe, and Asia for centuries, most of Africa south of the Sahara came into contact with Europe and Asia through the slave trade. The trade and the continual warfare which accompanied it weakened the highly developed native kingdoms in the Slave Coast, the Gold Coast, and Angola. When the time came for a confrontation with the European powers, most of these states collapsed. The modern nations of West Africa have not yet recovered from the blows of those centuries.

Most of the European slave-trading powers did not settle or colonize in Africa until the second half of the 19th century. Once established, the colonial system continued to stress the subservience of the black man, and, as a result, Africans did not become accustomed to working out their own destinies. The colonial system also allowed the natural resources of the continent to be taken, like the human cargoes before, to increase the wealth of European nations.

As we have suggested earlier, the evil influence of the slave trade was not limited to the continent of Africa. In the Western world, slavery and European colonialism in Africa were two of the major factors which contributed to the problem of racial discrimination and inequality in the modern era. The victim of racial discrimination is subjected to one of the most humiliating experiences in modern life, and the friction caused by such unfair treatment has become a serious problem in several parts of the world. In the

This black South African is breaking the law by sitting on a park bench reserved for Europeans (whites). If caught, he faces a fine of $20 or 20 days in prison.

United States, where slavery existed as an institution for many years, racial conflict has become a crucial national issue. In the Republic of South Africa and some other African countries, the colonial domination of a white minority over a black majority has been maintained in the face of growing resentment and threats of violence. Problems stemming from racial differences have also arisen within Great Britain, a nation which until recent years had a very small Negro population and considered itself free of the

disease of race prejudice. However, British antagonism to black immigrants from the Commonwealth's West Indian colonies has proved otherwise.

Discrimination against black people has taken many forms in 20th-century societies. Racial restrictions on personal freedom, jobs, housing, and education are applied informally in some countries, while in others the full powers of government legalize and enforce discriminatory treatment of Negroes. So long as black people in these various societies accepted the inferior position allotted to them, no problems arose. As the history of slavery itself has shown, however, a basically unjust system cannot survive indefinitely without being challenged. The challenge has been made and the old patterns of injustice are changing. In the United States the painful legacy of slavery has been finally and violently rejected; American Negroes are now fighting for the human rights which were denied them for too many years. They have been helped in their struggle by the example of black people in Africa who have asserted their own freedom and achieved independence from colonial rule. In some parts of Africa, however, the black man's rights are still withheld. Racial inequality has become a national policy in the Republic of South Africa, Rhodesia, and the Portuguese territories and is rigidly enforced by the ruling white minorities. The actions of the governments in these countries contrast sharply with the efforts of the United States government to bring about racial justice through law. Obviously, discrimination has not been eliminated in the United States, nor has the damage caused by past indifference been repaired. Much remains to be done before true racial justice is achieved, but the first steps have been taken.

Unlike the Europeans and Americans, the Arabs never completely stopped enslaving Africans even in the 20th century. Slave trading had become a way of life which some Arab countries were not prepared to give up. Perhaps if the European powers had held a better view of the human worth of black people, they could have put an end to all Arab slaving during the era of European colonialism in Africa. Be that as it may, there are indications that this last disgraceful example of an ancient evil will eventually die out in the modern world.

Martin Luther King leads participants in the March on Washington for Jobs and Freedom, August 1963. In his speech to the crowd gathered in front of the Lincoln Memorial, King spoke of his dream, "that one day this nation will rise up and live out the true meaning of its creed: 'We hold these truths to be self-evident, that all men are created equal.'"

History has shown us that any group of human beings can be discriminated against and even enslaved. In this century we saw how the Nazis forced people from Eastern Europe and Russia to serve as slave laborers during World War II. The brutal treatment given to Jews during this period is a notorious example of man's inhumanity to man. The sad story of cruelty and discrimination in human history should lead us to reflect that no one race or nation is immune to the possibility of mistreatment and humiliation at the hands of others. If we have no better reason for treating our fellow human beings with justice and compassion, then the lesson of history should be enough: what we do to others can easily be done to us.

Index

abolitionist movement: in Great
Britain, 79-86, 98-99; in U.S.,
111-115
Africa: effects of slave trade on,
122-124; European colonialism in,
96, 124; and illegal slave trade,
96; racial discrimination in, 125,
127; slavery in, 17-18; states of,
and European slave trade, 22-26
American Anti-Slavery Society, 112
Arab: exploration in East Africa,
67; slave coffles, 68; slave trade,
17, 21, 65-71, 127; systems of slavery, 69-70; trade in ivory, 67, 68
Ashanti, 25
asiento, 49

Benezet, Anthony, 74, 79
Brazil: abolition of slavery in, 120;
attitude toward Negroes in, 43,
46-47; and illegal slave trade, 92,
97; Portuguese heritage of, 43;
relations between races in, 45,
121; sugar plantations in, 44-55
British West Indies: abolition of
slavery in, 98-99; freeing of slaves
in, 53; slave laws in, 53-54; sugar
plantations in, 56-57

Christianity used as justification for
slavery, 10
Church of England, 9, 54-55
Civil War, U. S., 118
Clarkson, Thomas, 74, 79-84
clipper ships, 93
Code Noir, 58,59
coffee plantations, 47, 92
Coffin, Levi, 114

coffles, 33, 68
Compromise of 1850, 115, 117
Constitution, U. S.: references to
slavery in, 76-78; 13th Amendment of, 118
cotton gin, 91, 100
cotton plantations, 101, 103, 107, 108

Dahomey, 25, 85, 96
Danish West Indies, 59-60
Declaration of Independence, 75-76
Douglass, Frederick, 113
Dred Scott vs. *Sanford,* 117
Dutch colonies, 60-61

Elmina, 23, 33
Emancipation Proclamation, 118

Franklin, Benjamin, 74, 82, 87-88
freedmen, 14, 45, 53, 99, 111
French Revolution, 84
French West Indies, 58-59

Garrison, William Lloyd, 112, 113
Gold Coast, 23, 24, 25
Great Britain: abolitionist movement in, 79-86, 98-99; abolition of
slave trade in, 86; efforts of,
against illegal slave trade, 92-97;
and slave trade, 27-29, 82, 85-86
guinea, 28

Haiti, rebellion of slave in, 78, 84,
87, 89, 111

indentured laborers, 27, 29-32, 62
Indians, enslavement of, 48
Islam, 9, 21

The Author

L. H. Ofosu-Appiah is a native of Ghana, the modern West African nation which was once the Gold Coast. A distinguished scholar, teacher, and author, Dr. Ofosu-Appiah has pursued his academic career in schools throughout the world. He was educated at Achimota College in Ghana and at Oxford University in England, where he took degrees in classics and philosophy. He also attended Cambridge University and visited the United States as a Fulbright scholar. After teaching classics at the University of Ghana for 15 years, Dr. Ofosu-Appiah returned to the United States as a visiting professor and taught at Dartmouth College and Dillard University (New Orleans). Since 1966, he has served as director and editor of the *Encyclopaedia Africana*. Dr. Ofosu-Appiah has completed one volume of the *Encyclopaedia*, a collection of biographies, which will be published in the United States. Among his other scholarly works is a translation of Homer's *Odyssey* into Twi, a Ghanaian language. Dr. Ofosu-Appiah lives in Accra, Ghana, with his wife and three daughters.